Double Agent Marketing

"Live the Double Life, Control Your Destiny & Become a Self-Employed Entrepreneur by Starting Your Own Home-Based Internet Information Business"

By Robert Plank
www.DoubleAgentMarketing.com

© 2016 by Robert Plank, (408) 277-0904

Part 1: Work vs. Business

Chapter 1: Are You Too Busy Earning a Living to Make Real Money?

"A real entrepreneur is in it because she or he has no choice. They are dragged by their heart to build businesses and execute them. They aren't driven by the money or the current coolness of it. They do it because they have no choice, not because it's hot right now.
– Gary Vaynerchuk

I see many people hear about this thing called making money online, setting up an Internet presence, entering into niche marketing, affiliate marketing, product creation … and they "feel better" about passing along (parroting) what they've heard, instead of making money themselves. I hear cop-outs like "money isn't important to me" or "I'd rather change the world."

Look, making money online is SCARY!

Going into business for yourself is SCARY!

Controlling your own destiny is SCARY!

That's how things are. You've been conditioned throughout millions of years of evolution not to take risks, to blend, make friends, conform, play it safe, keep your head down, and survive.

And you've been taught all along that your life is supposed to go like this: go to school, go into debt, find a low paying job go into more debt, marry, have children, go into debt even further, try to save until age 60 or 70 (if you live that long), to possibly survive on a $1,000 or so per month fixed income.

IT'S THE "RETIREMENT MYTH!"

How does any of that make any sense?

I don't know whether you're young or middle aged and concerned about the future, if you're "over the hill" and possibly lost your job or lost your nest egg and you're trying to retrieve it , or you're old and don't have the 30 to 50 years you used to have at your disposal.

I'm not promising any kind of magic wand, magic button, magic bullet, or any other "instant" way out.

What will work? Starting your own business.

What's the cheapest and fastest way to start a business? The Internet. I'm talking about providing a service (like setting up websites for off-line businesses), or selling a digital product (like a home study course on how to flip real estate) – I'm talking about providing real value, solving people's problems with quick solutions. Your SYSTEM!

We're talking about you creating this thing called a "digital product" (e-book or membership site) that someone can buy and consume on autopilot. They need something from you, pay you for it, they download and use it, without you having to do anything.

There shouldn't be a difference if you make 10 sales or 1,000 sales or you need to take 1 day off your business or 30 days.

You'll need three things to have a full-time income established online: a web presence, an end-goal, and to make consistent progress daily.

Here are the three tools you'll use to make that possible (in the same order): an Income Machine system, a Double Agent Marketing strategy, and this productivity plan called Four Daily Tasks.

The "Income Machine" are the pieces of your online business that you'll have set up and working for you even when you're not at the computer, Double Agent Marketing is how you'll run a business without it hampering the rest of your life (or vice versa) and Four Daily Tasks is a simple time management plan that I use to ensure everything done that everything necessary was completed, without being distracted by the telephone, e-mail, or social media.

Chapter 2: Simple Questions to Ask Right Out of the Gate

"There are two rules for success: 1) Never tell everything you know."
– Roger H. Lincoln

I keep going back to this idea that "technically" you might have all the pieces in place. You have a sales letter with a headline that "should" work. You have a list and traffic. But you're still not making money.

Before putting your idea out to the marketplace, let's run it through this special filter to make sure we do as much as we can to guarantee it's a hot seller.

Question #1: Am I Solving a DESPERATE Problem?

This is no joke, and I feel bad for mentioning this person, but I said it was a bad idea than and I'll say it again now (ironically almost 9 years later) … someone once pitched a product idea to me basically to, "Quit your job in 9 years."

Not a year, not 6 months, 9 years. 468 weeks. 3,285 weeks. If you were 42 when you bought the course, congratulations, you can retire at 51. If your children were 6 and 10 when you started, now they're 15 and 19.

I suspect the product had something to do with budgeting, saving money, paying down debt, refinancing, consolidating, investing … although it might be good information, it's BORING! It's a not a hook, it's content you'd mention offhandedly in an info-product or a book, or better yet, at the beginning of a sales letter where you're explaining the solutions that NO ONE should try – like waiting 9 years for financial freedom. (Again, sorry if this is your product that I'm talking about.)

What's a better problem to solve? How about someone who wants to start stock options trading? Someone who has $10,000 cash in the bank (or a $10k loan) and wants to turn that into $15,000 or $20,000 or $100,000 in the next few months … can you show someone a "possible" way to do that? How to read charts, how to decide among stocks, options, bonds, mutual funds … how to diversify and invest safely?

Let me give you a few more "desperate" problems off the top of my head …

- How to attract a date in the next 7 days
- How to fix acne, tinnitus, yeast infections, hemorrhoids
- How to improve my vertical jump, golf swing, batting average
- How to manage stress, self-improvement, time management
- How to arrange an interview and a job
- Legal problems such as divorce, bankruptcy, traffic tickets
- Survive the recession, nuclear disaster, terrorist attack, civil war, and so on.

Does it fall into one of these three categories? Healthy, wealthy, or wise. AND … does it fit into one of the "seven deadly sins" from Catholicism? (lust, gluttony, greed, sloth, wrath, envy, pride)

This leads us to … not only is it a desperate problem, but also …

Question #2: Is the Problem & Solution Sexy?

You might say, I have a killer niche, Robert. It's how to achieve better grades in school ... and my answer to you is to achieve an A+ on that test, or achieving good enough grades for college ... really "sexy?"

Let's also think for a second about WHO will be buying this product. Definitely not the typical teenager. Most probably their parents are buying this course of yours, they hand it off to the child, and it is never opened or even used.

How about another idea ... musical instruments. "Some" musical instruments are excellent to teach online, because it's a skill that traditionally takes a long time and plenty of practice. Seeing a music tutor sucks because you have to schlep across town, you only see them once a week ... but if you have a SHORTCUT to conquer this skill in a short time, great!

But am I going to buy your course on how to play the trumpet? What about the tuba? Or the violin or clarinet or flute? Again, if I'm buying your course on how to play the trumpet I'm probably in the school band, in which case, my parent is making the purchase for me, in which case it's a small universe of people (children in the marching band whose parents also happen to buy your course.)

Let's go for a bigger audience ... how about someone learning to play the guitar? People of all ages learn to play the guitar, they're passionate about it, they're not playing just because they have to, but because they want to learn this skill and be cool.

Is marriage counseling a good niche? Again, if I'm having problems with my marriage I'll buy a $15 self-help book at the bookstore or on Amazon, or I'll see a license marriage counselor. I'm not going to buy your $97 (or higher) course online. What $30 e-book or $97 course will I buy? A "get your ex back" course!

Do you see a pattern here? If it's where someone might buy it as a gift, or something I have to work at for longer than a year, I'll look for the BORING solution off-line and not from you. But you can usually spin your idea into the "late-night infomercial" offshoot of it.

Question #3: Is the Solution Systematic or is It an "OR" Product?

We're talking about tips, tricks, hacks, and simple loopholes (which you don't want) versus systematic modules that take people from "point A to point B."

You've narrowed the niche you want into how to locate and attract your future husband in 30 days. Is this a situation where you can only list a few tips, for example, "30 Ways to Attract Your Future Husband" (a $10 book you read in the bathroom) ... or is it, "How to Attract Your Future Husband in 21 Days or Less" – now that's something that "could" be a book, but would work even better as a $97 or higher home study course.

Be careful about sharing various ways, approaches, and mistakes – a laundry lists of things you could do over here, or might do over there, and instead think about ... what do I want my buyer to achieve at the end of the 21 or 30 days? Great, that's the goal, now let's decide what steps need to be taken throughout.

Now I have a "system" that no one can copy. I can refer to this system almost as I refer to an appliance like a toaster, DVD player, iPhone, alarm clock. That's why I talk to you about the Four Daily Tasks method, or the Double Agent Marketing lifestyle, or the Income Machine system. I teach this black box and while others might have courses and training on time management, or on website creation, it's not quite the "Income Machine" system ... get it?

Question #4: Is There a "Future" in This Niche?

Some people recommend you find a way to make money from fads, for example, if some Internet legislation comes down the pipeline and you sell legal forms to website owners to become compliant. Or if Halloween is right around the corner so you set up websites selling Halloween costumes.

The problem with chasing these non-evergreen "fads" is that it's easy to make 10 or 20 dollars, but difficult to build a business with transactions of 100 dollars or more.

If you told me your niche was "back pain" ... my question to you would be, is that a niche where you could REALISTICALLY make money every month repeatedly? Or is this a situation where you sell an e-book for $10, which solves that person's problem, then there's nothing left to sell them because their problem is solved?

"Back pain" is too narrow a niche to run a whole business. But what if you were in the health niche and you had a product line devoted to solving your weight problem? With all the problems that come with extra weight. Just think bigger and create a $97 or $497 product that tackles not just back pain, but how to lose weight, how to lose fat, how to gain muscle, how to increase your energy, how to prolong your life ... THAT is where you'll see a continuing solution including dieting, exercise, and things like that.

A report on how to solve your anxiety, or how to increase confidence, is a pleasant start, but your own unique spin on HYPNOSIS or SELF-HELP is something where people will always need help, so you'll have an easier time making money.

Question #5: Is Someone in This Niche Willing to Raise Their Hand?

What if your idea was ... how to win at blackjack? What about ... how to become solvent? Yeast infections? Bladder problems?

Those are what you'd call "embarrassing" niches where people aren't willing to share with everyone.

Fortunately, weight loss and self-help are "cool" these days. The real test is, would you be embarrassed to tell your Mom, Dad, grandparent, or child that you bought a product in this niche? If someone had a similar problem as you, would you be willing to recommend this product as a solution?

There's an important reason that I ask this question and that's because, once your business is set up and online, you're going to want to start turning your buyers into affiliates. If someone bought your course, and you want them to recommend it to others, allow them to use their referral link so they can earn a commission if the sale comes from their Facebook page, blog, or e-mail list.

Looking back at some of these examples, what if your product was, for example, how to overcome your husband's addiction to pornography? That's not something you'd admit buying, certainly.

BUT! If you had a product that was a solution to addictions and destructive behavior, and was dedicated to overcoming bad habits like alcoholism, overeating, drama, gambling, pornography, drugs, smoking … people might be willing to admit they're a buyer EVEN IF you position it as a solution to their particular problem, if that makes sense.

Question #6: Am I Making This Too Complicated?

I'll never forget the first time Lance Tamashiro and I created a course together (years ago), and I'll never let HIM forget how silly it seems in retrospect. He had been one of my students for a while, but I didn't want to work with him.

He drew a series of boxes and arrows on a whiteboard, then filmed himself standing in front of it. He wanted to create a 4-week course called the "Blog Invasion System." It was a course about how to build reputation and authority, trust with your list, and become the expert in your field.

- Week 1 was the "Blog Makeover System" where you set up a blog if you don't already have one, with an opt-in form, pop-up box, comment capture, viral components, sticky components (like auto-sending e-mails to all commenters when there's a new blog comment)
- Week 2 was all about "Simple Joint Venture Tactics" like guest blogging, blog and ping, commenting on other blogs back to your site, making others notice you
- Week 3 was the "Automation" week where we taught people how to set up their blog to auto-blog about updates from other sites using RSS feeds, how to mine article sites

for content, pay for a steady stream of comments to keep the site fresh
- Week 4 covered "Long-Term Tactics" including video interviews, YouTube traffic, video testimonials

The course was a HUGE failure. We only sold 6 copies at $197 for the class ($1,152.95 total). The front-end videos and report, on a dime sale (price increases with every sale) only made us an additional $1,497.46 from 191 sales. $2,650.41 total from a multi-week launch. Not the huge payday we were looking for. For reference, I only consider a launch a "success" if it makes us $30,000 for STARTERS!

The reason for this failure? The problem wasn't urgent, it wasn't sexy and exciting, and it was on the vague side. Basically, we never should have done it. Instead, we should have created a class on something "proved" like copywriting, video, list building, or something similar.

The reason we finished by going ahead with the class was because we both fell in love with the "fanciness" of that funnel. Meaning, in the video Lance recorded to pitch me the idea, he structured it like this:

- People will come to the sales letter and see some text where we'll pitch a free video to them, then have to retweet the page to obtain access to the video
- That video will explain the OVERVIEW of this thing called the Blog Invasion System, and offer to show them the first video free, all they have to do is enter their e-mail address

- After entering their e-mail address, that first 5-minute video starts to explain the first part of the Blog Invasion System, then says ... if you want the videos and the report explaining the system, click here to pay $17
- After paying that $17 for the "5 Relationship Strategies", the web page said ... here are your videos but here is the $197 button to buy the live 4-week course

The moral of the story: you can have all the fancy funnels in the world but if your offer sucks, that isn't going to save it.

Even today, I see people who think that if they present their offer on an automated webinar, or on a Google hangout, or with a $7 price, $27 upsell, $17 down sell, that will save their offer. It won't. Radio announcer Ron Lyons coined this into a phrase in 1985 that's called, "Putting lipstick on a pig."

Question #7: Am I Searching for the Ideal Platform as a Reason Not to Start?

Because we mentioned things like automated webinars, let me round this out by telling you a huge stumbling blocks people have ... it's "searching for the ideal solution." Hint: there isn't one.

They're registered with five autoresponder providers yet they have no e-mail subscribers. Five shopping carts but they don't make any sales. They own five membership plugins but they don't have any members.

They want to run a webinar with 14 panelists that streams everyone's face, runs an unlimited number of attendees, and is FREE! Yet they haven't run a webinar of their own.

Look, if you need a domain name registrar and you don't have one, use NameCheap.com. If you need a web host, use HostGator.com. If you need an autoresponder, use Aweber.com. If you need a sales letter, use WordPress and PaperTemplate.com. If you need a way to take payments, use PayPal.com.

If you already happen to have a shopping cart or a membership plugin, then JUST USE WHAT YOU ALREADY HAVE! It is that simple. I know it doesn't "have to be" that simple, but let's make it that simple.

Once you've honestly answered these seven questions, we'll touch on the building of your business in the chapters ahead, notably *"How to Carve Your Own Niche"* and *"How to Pull Money Out of the Internet"* as well as the *"Double Your Income"* section, but DON'T SKIP AHEAD YET!

Chapter 3: Income Machine (Your Internet Presence)

"The secret of change is to focus all of your energy, not on fighting the old, but on building the new."
– Socrates

To have a completely automated Internet business you need these things: a niche (with a unique hook), a domain name, a website, an opt-in page, an e-mail autoresponder follow-up sequence, a blog, a sales letter with a product for sale, a membership site, and consistent traffic.

Many people just starting are stuck making $200 per month because they only have one piece of this set up. They send traffic to an affiliate link, make a few commissions, that's it. They've heard that "blogging" is a good idea, they post to their online journal several times a day just to earn a few dollars per day. They only have a SMALL PART of the whole system that they need …

Here is what you need and what you'll set up:

1. **Niche:** a "real" topic, audience and hook to base your business around
2. **Website:** a web address such as YourProductName.com
3. **Opt-in Page:** a simple web page where visitors can join your newsletter for a gift
4. **Follow-up Sequence:** a time-delayed series of e-mails, spread over several days
5. **Blog:** a public online journal such as YourProductName.com/blog or YourRealName.com

6. **Sales Letter:** a direct-response style web page with nothing other to do than buy
7. **Membership Site:** an area where your buyers can access downloads and watch videos
8. **Traffic:** a steady stream of visitors coming from free traffic (SEO) and paid traffic (PPC)

Those are the pieces that most of your competitors don't have, not powerful on their own, but working together, add to quite A LOT.

We have a training course showing you how to set it up at IncomeMachine.com. Once you have it set up then here's what happens:

- People on the Internet have a common problem: let's say they can't set up a WordPress blog, they can't lose weight, they search for solutions on forums, search engines, and on social media
- They find your paid Google advertisements, Facebook advertisements, retargeting advertisements, or possibly find your blog posts and articles in natural organic search-engine results, and visit your site
- They come click your opt-in page giving away a gift (on a site such as Example.com/free) on how to solve a simple weight loss problem
- After entering their name and e-mail address, they receive their report (and are now voluntarily opted in your e-mail mailing list, which they can leave at any time), and click your weight loss sales letter explaining the reasons you're different and convincing them that your product (your solution) is the answer to all their problems

- Even if they don't buy right away, your sequence continues following up with tips, advice, and help with their problems (all while whetting their appetite for your big solution)
- When it comes time for them to click and buy, they can enter their credit-card information and pay you automatically even if you're not at the computer, and access your member's area, again, even if you're not at the computer
- They can log in 24 hours a day to download your digital report, watch your online videos, and even buy other offers if they want (using the weight loss example: personal coaching, supplements, other reports)

It's agreeable to build some income this way but what your REAL goal is, what everyone wants whether they realize it, is this thing called a mailing list.

The Money Is in the (Targeted) List

Have you heard of the phrase, "The money is in the list?"

Even if you haven't, you build a big (targeted) list and you make big money. You don't build a list, you don't make money. You don't train your list to read, click, and buy … you don't make money. You don't build the relationship and earn your subscribers' trust … no money. You give away TOO MUCH free stuff without giving them real offers, no money.

Let's run a few numbers. You send 1,000 clicks (1,000 people) to that opt-in page. Let's say that traffic costs you 10 cents per click, meaning you spent $100 to obtain those 1,000 visitors.

On a simple opt-in page, you can expect 50% of people to register to claim their access to your free report. That means right off the bat, you lose 500 people (even if they are super-targeted) but you have 500 new people joining your e-mail list.

Many people won't even click to download that report. Even of those who do, many of them won't ever open the report to read it. Even of THOSE, 90% of them won't go past the first page. That's how the Internet is, people become distracted.

You should only expect 10% of those new subscribers to click from your "gift download" page (where they claim their free report) onto your sales letter (where they see an offer they can buy) – which means you obtain 50 clicks off the bat.

Now, how well is a sales letter supposed to "convert?" What percentage of people who visit your sales letter actually buy? It's hard to say, but a "typical" baseline is about 1 dollar per click, meaning if you're selling a short report for $17, expect it to convert at 5% or so. Sell a WordPress plugin for $47, expect it to convert at 2%. A home study course for $97, and 1%.

That means from those 1000 clicks, you achieve one sale at $47 ... therefore, you've paid $100 in advertisements and only made half your money back ... depressing right?

That's ONLY IF you market on the Internet the way most people do. Most people stop there and wonder why they lost money, why Internet marketing doesn't work, I wonder if there's any new reality TV on ...

You make your money back using what's called a 10-day follow-up sequence.

I just said people become distracted on the Internet. They might have been in a hurry, not ready to buy yet, not yet educated enough to make a buying decision, who knows why?

2% Click Through Rate

For every e-mail you send, you can expect about 2% of all subscribers to click through to your sales letter. That means your sequence contacts those subscribers once a day. The first few days, make sure they downloaded and consumed that free report, with a link to the sales letter too. Daily question them, let them know what's worked for you, and give them good reasons to examine your offer.

To obtain 1000 subscribers means you're sending 20 clicks to that sales letter daily. After 10 days, that's 200 clicks to your sales letter. If your sales letter converts at $47 at 2%, 4 sales from your sequence besides that sale you got right off the bat. 5 sales, $100 turned into $300.

Please note that I am sharing these figures "for entertainment purposes only" and I'm not guaranteeing any kind of income on your part. That's up to you. But this is the way you're going to think with the Internet. I have this offer, what am I selling it at, what price am I going to charge, how well is it going to convert, how big is my list, how much traffic am I sending to build that list?

I apologize if that was too much too fast, too money numbers thrown around but the point is to set up that Income Machine ... the blog, sales letter, opt-in page, sequence, everything ... so you can focus on TRAFFIC. Take that show on the road and rinse and repeat the process.

All the time, I run webinars (live streaming online presentations) for others free, because I want traffic. I'll publish books to bring traffic I'll speak on stages to bring traffic. Podcast episodes (iTunes radio) for traffic. Articles, blog posts, guest blog posts, Facebook advertisements, Google advertisements, all just to bring more TRAFFIC into the machine.

IMPORTANT: Now that your base system, your Income Machine is set up, you can focus on the "traffic tricks" (shiny objects) that you see all over the Internet. But don't go for any "cheap traffic tricks" until this Income Machine is in place!

Chapter 4: Double Agent Marketing (Manage It All)

"Too many people spend money they haven't earned, to buy things they don't want, to impress people they don't like."
– Will Smith

At this point, you're probably thinking, that sounds like a lot of stuff to set up, many things to learn, and much trial and error, how am I going to have time for all that? I have a job, or I'm a student, or I'm a single mother, or I'm a dad with four children, or I've got a demanding job that requires 60 hours a week, or I'm retired but I'm on a fixed income and I don't have the time or energy to put in long hours as I used to when I was 20.

That's fine. The first thing you need to do is manage your day job and your online business. Keep them entirely separate, and knock out your tasks in a short time (because you have no other choice).

We've all experienced that lost weekend where we started playing on Facebook, bought a batch of $5 courses, set up some advertising accounts, bought into a biz-opportunity, bought resale rights, played on some advertisement network, decided it was time to learn web programming … "went down the rabbit hole" … and blew throughout a weekend ignoring friends and family, not showering, hardly eating, never seeing sunlight …

Doing "work." Wasting "time." Nothing to show for it.

It's a basic time management problem. If you don't know what your goal is, you have nothing to develop, then you'll let yourself become distracted by every shiny object that comes your way.

When most people have other commitments, they see it as a disadvantage but it's actually an advantage.

There's a reason that you goofed off in high school, college, teenage years, early 20s … you had a lot more time than money, no one depending on you, nothing to lose.

The idea of making $1,000 or $10,000 or $100,000 or $1,000,000 or millions or tens of millions of dollars online sounds okay, but what will that bring you? More "stuff?" A sports car that you can't drive anywhere (it might be scratched) that you can barely afford payments on? A big house with 10 bedrooms, more than you would ever use?

How about … instead of striving towards a number, or collecting "stuff" … you could retire a decade earlier than you previously thought? You paid off your cousin's mortgage? Sent your daughter to college? Set up a charity? Traveled around the world?

Money is an "okay" motivator. But what's even more powerful and emotional is WHAT YOU'LL DO once you have that money. People in self-help call this your "reason-why."

Not only do you need to use your family and your well-being as your motivator, you need to keep your home life and business life SEPARATE. When you're building your business, you're 100% focused. When you're spending time with your family, you're 100% focused on that.

I know, in this day-and-age where texts are always popping up and all your friends are just a Facebook click away, this seems impossible, but what we want to do with our "Double Agent Marketing" lifestyle is to sit at our "hot seat" computer and complete our tasks as fast as possible.

That means don't open e-mail, don't open Facebook, and don't check text messages until you're done.

Here's what you'll need to live a Double Agent Marketing lifestyle:

Component #1: Automate What Needs Automating

This first seems simple to most Internet-savvy geeks but most of us don't do it – and we need to. Set as many everyday tasks as you can on automatic pilot. That means set up your phone bill, electricity bill, gas bill, cell-phone bill, mortgage, day care, car payment, and live below your means.

Component #2: Gmail

"Traditional" e-mail works like this: set up a desktop program like Outlook, leave it open in the background so it "dings" every time a new message rolls in. Your inbox grows to 5000 … 10,000 … 100,000 unread messages. You're almost "chained" to the computer because you can't easily check e-mail from the road. And good luck moving your e-mail if you buy a new computer!

Here's a better solution: Google Mail or Gmail. It's web-based, you can access it from anywhere, you "label" e-mails (instead of moving them to folders), it groups messages into "conversations", and you archive mail or delete it.

Unread or unreplied e-mail is in your inbox. Once you're done with it, you can click a button to "archive" that e-mail (or back-and-forth conversation). It's out of the Inbox but available in the "All Mail" section and it's still searchable.

Instead of riffling through thousands of messages, I usually have 100 or fewer e-mails in my inbox (on a good week), sometimes 100 to 500 e-mails (if I haven't checked e-mails in a while) but never more than 500.

Out of all the possibilities I've tried, this is the best way to manage piles of e-mail without it taking your life over.

Component #3: Google Calendar

When you receive a Gmail account (free), you also receive this thing called "Google Calendar" that you can also access from anywhere, which syncs up to your smart phone or tablet. That means you set an appointment on your phone, and you can access it from your laptop or your computer.

You can also share your calendar with other users. I have my calendar, my business partner Lance Tamashiro has his calendar, he has a calendar for his family, and we have a shared calendar.

When we need to meet, or run a session for one of our classes, a coaching or Q&A session, it's on the calendar days or weeks before time. That means I can wake in the morning, check the calendar to see where I need to be, and not have to keep my phone on to risk being interrupted.

Component #4: Countdown Timer or Camtasia Babysitter

You've got a handle on e-mail and other interruptions, let's talk about you knocking out those tasks. You have a niche and a domain name set up, now it's time to create an opt-in page to give away a free report for a first name and e-mail address ...

You start with a blank piece of page on your computer and you think ... I need a good headline. Let me go post on a forum and ask about good headlines to use. While I'm there I'm going to read a few other topics about things like Fiverr, LinkedIn, and PerfectAudience, whatever those are. I wonder if Facebook has any good suggestions. Now that I'm on Facebook I wonder what some of my friends are doing. Hey, this looks like a fun game to play on Facebook. My Facebook is already open, so why not YouTube? Let me check my blogger feed.

Do you see what happened? You let yourself take a tiny peek, a baby step, and it snowballed into a huge time distraction. You thought you were smarter than the system when the system was actually smarter than you.

Here's a weird way to keep yourself on task that shouldn't work, but does: equip yourself with a countdown timer. On Windows, I use a cool called "Cool Timer" but on a Mac, you can use a web-based version at Online-Stopwatch.com.

If that opt-in page is going to take you 15 minutes, set the timer to count your 15 minutes and you do NOTHING else until that's done. You don't have time to check e-mail and Facebook, you've got a deadline coming! Once your 15 minutes are up, you're off the computer and off to real life.

And even on those rare days when the countdown timer fails, I'll open a screen recording tool called Camtasia and literally RECORD the actions I'm taking on my screen to ensure I don't move off-task.

Component #5: Accountability Partner

People who fail at marketing (especially on the Internet) are those who try to go it alone. I'm not JUST talking about hiring people for the tasks you can't do or don't want to do, I'm talking about a "personal" support system.

Don't confuse the term "support system" with something like a "customer support desk." I'm talking about your allies, people who will support you, and not just your friends and family. If you're like me and you want to run a business on the Internet, you're going to quickly discover that hardly anyone in your life "gets it."

They'll make fun of what you do, they won't respect your time, and say discouraging things especially if the money doesn't come in right away. (Never mind that most off-line business require huge loans to start and take at least 5 years to turn a profit.) You'll almost feel like an alien from space, setting your own hours and "working" when and where you want while they're all confined to cubicles from 9am to 5pm.

That's where an accountability partner comes in. Someone you MIGHT have as a business partner, but even if they aren't, we're talking about a person you can report to whether you completed your tasks for today.

Here's how I started with it: I'd call up a friend (it was the same person daily) in the morning to list off the things I wanted to do that day. I'd call back in the afternoon and went down the list. I did this, I finished that (feeling good as I was saying it), but I didn't finish that for this reason (feeling bad about having an excuse). This simple but useful tool "connected" those logical things I knew I should do, with the emotional drive needed to do it quickly.

Chapter 5: Four Daily Tasks (Consistent Daily Follow-Through)

"Successful people are simply those with successful habits."
– Brian Tracy

Because we're on staying productive and progressing daily, here's the template that works: Four Daily Tasks. It seems almost TOO simple, and that's why many people overlook it, but if you can find a way to move past it, this will work wonders, I promise you!

The End of To-Do Lists

Let's think for a second about what DOESN'T work. First, you might have tried these things called "To-Do Lists."

What was that really? It was a laundry list of 100 things (or more) that needed to be done. Taxes, check social media, set up AdWords account, clean toilet, call Jimmy, check e-mail, check voicemail, check snail mail, mow lawn, clean gutter, clean desk, clean office, vacuum, set up affiliate program … what a mess!

The problem with leaving things unstructured in this way is that you'll have days where you complete 20 items, days with 0 items, weeks where you're burned out and useless. You'll cross off 10 items and add 20 more. You'll find yourself SLOWING your productivity down the closer you are to finishing!

Look, knocking out just one daily task with no clean plan doesn't work, but "chipping away" on a large problem does not work either! I've tried all the systems. I've tried the ones where you separate your to-do list items into quadrants. I've tried the one where you schedule your free time (and even bathroom breaks) into your calendar – doesn't work. I've tried the one where you list all your tasks into columns in a spiral bound notebook. And I've tried the WORST of them all, not having a time management system!

Can I tell you what does work? Are you open to it? It's called Four Daily Tasks. Have four manageable tasks you'll complete that day.

We're talking three 45 minute tasks and one 15 minute task and THAT'S IT! You might underestimate yourself and finish all four in an hour, or before lunch, then you're done for the day!

You DON'T need to confuse and complicate it by "adding to this." You DON'T need to say, I'll have four tasks, but I'll always set this one task to be the one I do first. You DON'T need to say, I'll have four tasks, plus 10 micro-tasks or "grout" that I'll fill throughout the day as needed. You DON'T need to say, I'll complete 20 small things instead of 4 medium-sized things. True, you might have to chunk tasks together and dedicate a 45-minute session to traffic by posting articles, tweaking Facebook advertisements, updating your fan page, running some retweets, inviting people to Google-Plus events, but that's a 45-minute task and not twenty 5-minute tasks.

What you CAN do is combine the earlier techniques we talked about like Gmail, Google Calendar, countdown timer and accountability partner to ensure you complete all four tasks of the day. And you know what? If you're new to this you probably aren't yet "calibrated" and can't properly estimate how long 45-minutes is, and might only be able to complete 2 out of 4 tasks.

For example, if you're new to setting up web pages or opt-in pages, this actually might be a 2-hour long process. Does that mean you do it in 2-hours? Of course not! Your day might look like this:

1. Set up Paper Template plugin on new domain. (45 minutes)
2. Write headline and bullet points for opt-in page. (45 minutes)
3. Create web form and download page. (45 minutes)
4. Test opt-in and add first welcome e-mail. (15 minutes)

You set, and arrived at, clear milestones to reach where you wanted to go.

Let's be honest. You won't always complete your 4 tasks for today, but that doesn't mean you'll go with 5 tasks or 6 tasks tomorrow. It means you still only have 4 tasks to complete tomorrow!

That means you'll need to move the tasks you didn't complete to tomorrow's tasks (let's say you didn't finish two things, now you'll finish those and complete two more). OR maybe those tasks you missed today weren't important and you don't need to work on them yet!

The Google Calendar keeps us on track with deadlines and product launches coming up so many times, I'll progress on to something that's now a huge priority (like a book) that will have to go to the wayside to launch a product or run a class. Then, weeks or months later, that book might return on the radar and it'll become part of my tasks again.

By the way, if you're having trouble knocking out these tasks, we have a private group on Facebook that you can join. The URL to join is: http://www.fourdailytasks.com/group and many of us (including Lance and I) post there daily. We abbreviate website and product names to avoid revealing anything confidential, but the act of posting our list, and knowing that people will read that list, keeps us on track.

Seriously. When I notice I haven't been productive in a few days, it's because I've stopped posting my Four Daily Tasks, and when I've noticed I've been on a roll, it's because I've been sticking to my Four Daily Tasks.

One final thing. These are BUSINESS related tasks. Exercise, meditation, waiting for things like traffic and sales, wrapping Christmas presents, attending birthday parties, are all PERSONAL items that shouldn't be organized, that I shouldn't know about. When we're talking about four daily tasks, these are business related activities, clear milestones that you could literally show me were completed.

You're Standing in An Airplane ...

If you were standing at the door of a (small) airplane at 10,000 feet in the air and the airplane was ON FIRE and about to crash ... you have a parachute on your back, the choices are no longer:

- **Option #1:** not to jump and live a life of safety
- **Option #2:** jump out of the plane and parachute down

The choices have now become ...

- **Option #1:** DIE
- **Option #2:** jump and parachute to safety

Why did I ask such a silly question and what's my point?

Launching a product. Putting something out there. Running a 1-hour pitch to an audience if that's what you want. USING that GoToWebinar account if you have one. USING that automated webinar tool if you have one. I can't believe I'm about to say this, but USING Google Hangouts if that's the direction you're going ...

If you have something that works, if you're 99% to the finish line, why stop now?

The way I see it ...

Option #1: don't run webinars, don't launch your products, remain a "sheepish" dabbling shy marketer (trust me if anyone suffers from "shyness" it's me so I'm right there with you), don't make as much money as you could, don't live up to your potential and wonder how it could have been

Option #2: make a wad of money in 60 minutes, be proud of what you've achieved, repeat the process and return to what matters in life (while your websites and videos continue to attract traffic and income on autopilot)

Look, do you want a "full-time income" (12-14 hour days for $30k a year or less like some people are proud of) or do you want an appointment-based business where you show up, do your thing, and you're back to HOBBIES, HAVING FUN, and staying off the computer?

I don't know about you, but that sounds good to me.

Part 2: Work vs. Family

Chapter 6: Put on Your Oxygen Mask

"When your life flashes before your eyes, make sure you've got plenty to watch." – Anonymous

You need to put on your oxygen mask before helping others.

I don't know whether you've heard that saying, but it means, if you're sitting in an airplane about to crash, and the oxygen masks drop, you're supposed to put the mask on YOURSELF before helping your next-door neighbor in the seat next to you, or even children.

I'm mentioning that metaphor to you because I see way too many people "martyr" themselves and I don't want you to fall into that trap. What am I talking about? I'm talking about people who feel as if they have to suffer so they can improve the life of others.

- "Money isn't important to me. I just want to spend my time helping others, and that's why I'm posting and lecturing on message boards all day instead of setting up websites."
- "I don't want to quit my job, I don't want a $1000 per month income. I just want an extra $100 per month or $1000 per year to buy Christmas presents."
- "I want to start a business of my own but I don't have the time to do it, so I'm going to stay at the job I hate so I can provide for my family."

Look, I understand you have a family and that it comes first and that you'd do anything for them … but if you want a better life for yourself and for them, why don't you risk it?

Between work and a business, there is a difference. "Work" means you aren't in control, someone else decides what you wear, where you go, when you go there and how much you're paid. It also means they can kick you out at any time, it doesn't matter how "secure" you think your job is. Even tenured teachers can become fired.

I think that if you WANT to be an entrepreneur, or if you've got something going already, that you need to build a business and phase out "work" for your family's sake.

The thing we call a "reason-why" is the best motivator. Money on its own is not a good motivator. The things you can buy with money (an expensive car to show off to your friends, a house that's too big with the attic crammed full of stuff you don't need) doesn't sound like a good goal. You know what does sound like a good goal?

It's the answer to this question: "What are you going to do AFTER you make enough money to retire? I asked this to a few hundred people (my e-mail subscribers) and here were the answers:

- 11.61% said, "spend more time with family"
- 12.50% said, "volunteer"
- 18.75% said, "relax and retire"
- 26.79% said, "travel"
- 30.36% said, "build a business"

Please note that when I asked this, it wasn't "multiple choice" or anything like that, it was open ended. People typed in any response they wanted, and when I categorized the responses ... **THESE WERE THE ONLY FIVE VARIATIONS!** Out of several hundred of responses.

This tells us a few things: first, that if you haven't developed your reason-why yet, one of these options will easily jump out at you – remembering that people with families who said they'd "travel" PROBABLY meant "travel with family."

Look, if you have a family, I understand that you're short on time. But if you're using your family as an excuse, I'm going to tell you that you're only hurting yourself!

It's a time management problem. I know plenty of people with several children, newborn children (like Lance Tamashiro) who "work" FAR LESS HOURS than people with only one child, or full-grown children who have long moved out ... so what's the secret?

The first is that appointment-based business we discussed earlier. Seriously, set up a Google Calendar for your business, set one up for your significant other, and schedule in school sporting events, parent teacher conferences, field trips, your day job if you still have one, webinars you're going to run, whatever needs to be managed.

Leave plenty of room between meetings to make sure you're early for everything. Also take advantage of 5 minutes here and there. Let's say you're waiting to collect Suzie from day care at 4PM. Plan to arrive there at 3:45 and while you're waiting in your car, type a quick sales letter or send out a broadcast e-mail to your list.

This also makes sure you aren't glued to the computer and that you miss family time.

The second is to cut TV time. This is the easiest low-hanging fruit to release extra time. Don't believe me? Examine the results of this study conducted by the Nielsen Company back in 2013:

- Children aged 2-11 watch **24 hours per week**
- Teenagers aged 12-17 watch **22 hours per week**
- Adults aged 18-24 watch **24 hours per week**
- Adults aged 25-34 watch **29 hours per week**
- Adults aged 35-49 watch **34 hours per week**
- Adults aged 50-64 watch **44 hours per week**
- Adults 65 and older watch **49 hours per week**

No matter what your age, if you quit watching TV immediately, you'd free the equivalent of a full-time job. I know, I know, many of you would rather lose an arm rather than give up TV. But what if you could break that vicious circle of …

- Wake
- Go to work
- Watch TV
- Go to sleep

… And you replaced "watching TV" with reading a book, family time, record 1 extra video for my course, run 1 pitch webinar to make extra sales, recruit some new affiliates, manage pay-per-click advertisements, ghostwrite articles for clients?

I have been off live TV for over a decade now. I still go to the movies, I still watch DVDs, I have a Roku player (similar to Apple TV), which streams Netflix, Hulu Plus, and Amazon Instant

Videos to my TV. It can also stream iTunes purchases from the Media Center on my computer. I can watch TV, I just have to pay for what I watch, there are little commercials, I can't flip channels, and when the episodes over, I'm done with TV.

Maybe you could decide to only watch TV on weekends? Or quit TV for 7 days or 30 days while you spent time on your business … you know, working to quit your job so you could make a better life for you and your family?

I know the answer seems too simple. But if live TV sucks up too much time, and you decide you don't want to watch live TV, then don't have live TV in the house!

(If you want to lose weight, don't have junk food in the house!)

This brings me to my third point, avoid becoming a martyr. I have friends who had children by accident, and thus were poor and stretched for time working several jobs, and others who planned their children. I see a common factor. They're busy and if I can be blunt, they use their children as excuses slightly more often than they should. They're so busy, there's no time to even start about creating a business, and then … they'll watch TV for hours.

They use that they have a family to say … I don't have enough time to work a day job and spend time with my family and build this thing called my own business. I didn't say it would happen overnight. But what you're working towards is to make MORE money in less time by working from home. Even the time you save commuting is huge.

You'll self-sabotage your efforts if you let yourself. Without a plan, your "busy time" is going to inflate to match the amount of "free time" so make the schedule work. These hours I'm at my day job, these hours I'm building my business, the rest is family time. Will you have to hire a babysitter to watch the children while you build your business? Maybe, but figure it out!

Fourth, set a real quitting date for when you want to quit that job to go full-time AND have a real list of criteria that you'll need to quit.

If you think you'll wake one day and just quit, without planning whatsoever, you're wrong. I think it's true that you'll have those days when you're ready to cut the cord and put in your two weeks' notice. But I also think you'll chicken out (as I sometimes did) unless you have a LOGICAL checklist completely checked off (as I did).

- What exact date do I plan to quit?
- Do you have health insurance set up?
- Do you have set hours for building your online business?
- How much cash flow would have to be coming in per month?
- How much cash is in the bank to cover emergencies?
- Based on these numbers, how much time have I to make this happen?
- What is my backup plan in case I need to find emergency income? (such as freelancing)

Either way, you're going to kiss your job good-bye. After you quit, good luck achieving that old job back 6 months or a year later. Answer those seven questions REALISTICALLY and you're on your way.

In addition, be prepared for this to strain your family and your marriage – as any big change will do. But if you see it coming, I think it'll be worth it.

In a while, we'll discuss that you never put in an "8 hour day" – it's mostly wasted time – so when you're working full time for yourself, you'll be able to complete an entire day in 15 minutes to 2 hours.

If you absolutely had to run a business on just 1-2 hours a day at the most, you could find a way to do it – probably by closing distractions like e-mail, cell phones, social media, and live TV … it's all about removing BOTTLENECKS!

Let's look at real data instead of just guessing. At one point, I asked my subscribers, "What takes up most of your time … what's stopping you from making a lot of money in a short time … what's your biggest bottleneck?" And here were the answers:

- 14% said **money or cash flow**
- 20% said **time management, day job or children**
- 20% said **confidence, faith, completion, the big picture**
- 23% said **focus, distractions, discipline, mentorship**
- 23% said **technical details**

Remember again, I categorized the free-response answers and that these rounded-off numbers come from hundreds of real answers. These five responses are evenly spaced out, but the good news is, if you fix just ONE of these problems, you're 20% of the way to having everything solved. I'm going to give you the "quick answer" to each of these common problems …

Solution to your cash flow problem: Live below your means.
This means reduce your bills somehow so you're paying down
your debt monthly (or don't have debt), cook meals at home
instead of drinking Starbucks every morning and eating out every
night. Buy a used $20,000 or $30,000 car instead of leasing an
$80,000 car. Live in a 2-bedroom apartment instead of a 4-
bedroom or a $400,000 house instead of an $800,000 house (both
keep out the rain just as well!)

The important thing is to have a budget and manage your money so
you're ideally putting away AT LEAST $1,000 per month into a
savings account. If you have to swallow your pride and use your
spouse to attract a second income for the good of the family, do it!

**Solution to your time management problem: Set up rules,
structure and extinguish fires before they spread.** When I
observe couples where one is the "day job worker" and the other
tries to make it online, I see quite a bit of resentment. One person
always thinks they're working harder and usually it's the one going
into work daily! Chances are they think, "You're goofing off at
home on the computer playing Solitaire" … when you're trying to
build a business. You don't have to suffer at the computer for 8
hours, but show your daily task list to your spouse.

Show how you're building that list. And at first, if you have to
freelance a job on sites like oDesk writing articles, transcribing
audios, answering telephone customer support for others … just to
have "some" money coming in to prove this Internet thing makes
money … DO IT!

Something else that was a HUGE help: adjusting my day job
hours. On a typical day, I'd be at the office 8PM to 5PM with two
15-minute breaks and a 1-hour lunch break. But we could work a

few things out where I'd come in at 10AM on some days and stay until 6:30PM with a half-hour lunch break, and other days where I was in my office at 6AM and could leave at 2:30PM with a half-hour lunch break.

The 6-2:30 schedule was ideal. I'd be home before 3 and it felt like having an extra day to build my business! I'd hustle through the things I needed to do and hit the gym before 5. It's all about time management and having a schedule that fits your lifestyle.

Solution to your confidence and big picture problems: Choose a role model and discover what that person did to achieve the same result as you want. We've all experienced analysis paralysis, overwhelmed with so many choices. You don't know how to position your WordPress product? What price to charge, what to include in the offer? Look at the other popular products on WordPress, even buy those products, and MODEL what worked in your own way with your own unique twist. (Notice I didn't say, "Copy.")

Solution to your focus problems: Complete your tasks in short bursts and chunk smaller tasks together into 45-minute ones. You don't need to check e-mail several times a day. You probably don't need to check social media more than once a week. And even when you do, I would lump all your social media together so you're checking Facebook messages, Facebook advertisements, sending tweets, managing that LinkedIn group, all in one 45 minute session, then you're DONE! No checking back to do one more thing. You can log back on when it's an "official" task for the day.

Studies have shown repeatedly that when you hear a text message sound, or a Facebook status update rolls in, or heck, you BUY something online, your brain gives you a small dopamine boost. This means that you are probably physically and chemically addicted to your cell phone.

If you don't believe me ... how many times have you thought you felt a vibration on your phone but nothing came in? Or you were driving somewhere and you turned around to go BACK home to collect your cell phone? I hate to sound dramatic, because it's not life threatening, but it is an addiction. You need to become used to shutting off your phone and placing it out of reach while you have these focused sessions so you can actually concentrate for longer than two minutes at a time.

Solution to your technical details: Join a course (to solve big problems) or watch YouTube (to solve small problems). Here's the thing. If you or I want to learn a new skill, we're going to either have to pay time or money for it. People who don't understand this are those who spend a year (or longer) trying to piece together things like "how to set up a membership site" instead of buying a course and figuring it out within a few days or less.

When I tell you to join a course, I mean to treat it like school. As if you have a pop quiz coming up later. That means buy a course with video, and watch the videos all the way through, paying 100% attention (no multi-tasking or pausing) until you understand it. Then, go back through the videos (a second pass-through) and carefully set up the membership site as you follow along, WITHOUT deviating or becoming bored/distracted as I see so many people do.

Likewise, to solve smaller problems, 5-minute problems instead of 5-hour ones, search YouTube for the problem you're trying to solve. Years ago, I was trying to figure how to create green screen video just as they do on the news. I searched "green screen video" and after having a few false-starts, I found a 5 minute video created by a 12 year old showing how to do the lighting, backdrop, and the most important part, what software and what menus in the software to achieve the desired effect.

Some problems are "join membership" problems, some are "search YouTube" problems and the rest are problems where I ask, "Do I need to know this? Am I going to let this problem delay me for several days? Will doing this make me more money or am I using it as an excuse?"

For example, I have seen many people ask how to add 1-click upsells to their sites. How to drip membership content. How to split test the e-mails they send out. How to send direct mail pieces using snail mail. If you don't have the simple things online yet (like a basic website or sales letter with a payment button) then you don't NEED the advanced stuff yet!

You can solve most of these problems by adopting an ENTEREPRENEURIAL MINDSET as opposed to the EMPLOYEE MINDSET, which you'll have to unlearn over the next few weeks. Keep reading to discover what I mean …

Chapter 7: Employee Mindset

"Normal is getting dressed in clothes you buy for work and driving through traffic in a car that you are still paying for - to get to the job you need to pay for the clothes and the car, and the house you leave vacant all day so you can afford to live in it."
— Ellen Goodman, American journalist

Quick question: **do you believe that being rich, or poor, is a choice?**

That's a rude question to ask, but think about your answer. Donald Trump has billions of dollars, do you think he just lucked into it?

You might say that Trump's father was wealthy and that's why The Donald is wealthy. But isn't it possible that he could have spent all that money? You might also say, but Robert, don't you know that Donald Trump has filed for bankruptcy twice? True, his companies have filed bankruptcy so they could restructure, but he was still able to rebuild it and still has a heck of a lot more money than you. (No offense.)

Look at people like Larry King, Steve Jobs, and George Foreman who lost everything and could rebuild it. Then compare them to the typical jackpot lottery winner who ends in MORE debt than they were before they won their money.

Your mindset plays a huge part in how much money you'll make, how quickly, and whether you'll keep your money once you earn it. I guess you could say that "luck" is also a factor, but the good thing about luck is that you have several chances to get it right. I think that losing all your money is a RITE OF PASSAGE and is a required step to making the sum and cash flow you deserve and desire.

Look, at some point you were someone else's employee. You had to be somewhere when they said you had to be there (maybe you were on-call), you were paid how much "they" decided you were worth, "they" even decide when you've outlived your usefulness!

Even as a young child, I remember my Dad working for 3M. He developed some electronics "thing" (I was too young to know what), at home, during his time, but because of his contract, they owned the rights, and not him. I had a friend out of college who worked for, let's call it Company #1, but was subcontracted out to Company #2. This person "earned" $9 per hour, but Company #2 paid Company #1 $12 per hour. How much sense does that make? None!

All of us know "that person" who felt as if they had to play by the rules. High school, college, career, wife, children, retirement, right? Wait till age 65 and "hope" nothing goes wrong.

On the other end, the Internet marketing niche is littered with so-called "misunderstood geniuses." The ones who say, "I never went to college because I heard it was a waste of time."

Whether you did or didn't go to college, whether you think that you need college or you don't, that's your opinion. I don't think college is a nice-to-have, it's a must-have especially so you have more employment opportunities to support yourself and your family while your business take off from the ground.

Bill Gates and Mark Zuckerberg dropped out of Harvard because their business TOOK OVER! If you had to develop Microsoft BASIC or Facebook, and it was a time management problem, you'd drop out too.

You know what else? Gates and Zuckerberg had to enter Harvard to drop out.

My point? Don't drop out of school, don't quit your job tomorrow just because you want to start a new business. Start the business, run with it, and when it overtakes everything else, THEN it's time to drop out.

That's why we're calling this "Double" Agent Marketing. For a while, you WILL have to pursue these parallel lives to build your future.

Hopefully you aren't in a career where "they" own your intellectual property. BUT! When I worked for California State University Stanislaus, I carefully looked over my contract and noticed a few things:

- Using my office space for personal meetings, not allowed
- Using my telephone for anything other than "occasional use" outside work, not allowed
- Using my computer or Internet access for non-work activities, not allowed

The good news was that I was in a career COMPLEMENTARY to my Internet business. Meaning, I had skills like web programming, C++, Java, PHP, JavaScript. I made sure to obtain a job also in web programming. They trained me in NEW areas like jQuery,

Perl, SharePoint, Oracle, and Microsoft SQL Server. This was necessary training for my job.

Did I build my business during office hours? Heck no. But did I use what I learned to create products and training in my business? You had better believe it! You know what else? I started waking an hour early (so I would have 1 hour before work for business building), I rearranged my work schedule so on SOME days I could come in from 6AM to 2:30PM.

And the biggest boost? I learned, and applied, good time management in my business, because I had no other choice!

The Sad but True Reality of the Employee

Here's the schedule of a "typical" employee:

- 7:00 AM: Wake
- 7:30 AM: Leave for work
- 8:00 AM: Arrive at work
- 8:10 AM: Co-worker talk
- 8:15 AM: Bathroom/coffee
- 8:20 AM: Turn computer on
- 8:30 AM: Sit at computer
- 8:45 AM: Phone rings
- 9:00 AM: Coffee break
- 9:15 AM: Bathroom break
- 10:00 AM: Morning break
- 10:20 AM: Back from break
- 10:30 AM: Bathroom again
- 10:45 AM: More coffee
- 11:00 AM: Check e-mail
- 12:00 PM: Lunch break
- 1:15 PM: Return a little late
- 1:30 PM: Bathroom break
- 1:45 PM: Coffee break again
- 2:00 PM: 15 minutes of work
- 2:15 PM: Interruption
- 3:00 PM: Afternoon break
- 3:30 PM: Become settled
- 4:00 PM: Check e-mail
- 4:30 PM: Wind down
- 5:00 PM: Finish with work
- 5:30 PM: Leave for car
- 6:00 PM: Arrive home tired
- 6:30 PM: Switch on TV
- 7:00 PM: Dinner
- 7:30 PM: More dinner
- 8:00 PM: More TV
- 9:00 PM: Think about exercise but forget
- 10:00 PM: Sleep

The point of all this is that your typical day is filled with "activity" ... busy-ness instead of business, running out the clock. Because you are paid regardless! You only put in 15 minutes of work, and you're actually TRAINED to be inefficient, because your co-workers work slowly AND you want to manage expectations. If you start knocking tasks out at a breakneck pace, people will become used to it!

A good thing about working at a day job: it's a steady paycheck, it's "safety" (at least for a while), it gives you something to "hate" (a life of mediocrity you want to escape), and you can finally realize that in any day, you only achieve 15 minutes of. Think about that. 8 hours wasted (9 if you count your commute), only 15 minutes of productivity.

There's "employee" you and "entrepreneur" you. "Employee" you can clock in and clock out, and waste time, but when you're in business for yourself, there's no point in dragging your feet the way you're used to doing it!

Most people don't realize this is what they're doing. They have some limiting belief that time equals productivity equals money. Not necessarily. You can't put in 12-14 hour days, for 10 years, and expect to "pay your dues" and receive your money. The REALITY is that you don't have to suffer, and that if you had to, you could survive on 15 minutes per day.

If you have a day job or other obligations, and the ONLY time you could squeeze in was one hour on your lunch break, one hour in the morning, or one hour in the evening, you could make it happen.

The first thing you need to focus on is set up your Income Machine (niche, website, opt-in page, follow-up sequence, blog, sales letter, membership site) and once that's done, it's joint ventures and traffic to attract consistent sales.

Break the usual pattern of Work-TV-Sleep and build that business that serves a real need, brings traffic, builds a list, converts prospects into sales, and gives you extra income.

You have a choice between a "scarcity" mindset and an "abundance" mindset. Scarcity means that everyone's out to screw me, I need to scrimp, save, and hoard all my money into a savings account.

Or you can choose the better way the "abundance" mindset. I'm out to help people, without giving everything away free, without being a martyr, without being one of those "afraid of money."

Here's the thing. Let's say you teach real estate, specifically how to buy and flip homes. From your point of view, it's borderline DISGUSTING that some people lose money with real estate. It's DISGUSTING that people out there try to teach it without doing it, who share outdated methods or things that just plain don't work.

Or you teach how to trade stock options. The typical person is going about it wrong. They're listening to the wrong people, making all the mistakes. You have a better way.

Isn't it true that if someone asks you something such as … "How do I lose 20 pounds for my wedding, happening in 30 days?" And you're a weight loss expert, you could give someone a 3-minute answer, a 45-minute answer, and a 4-hour answer?

For the 3-minute answer: you only have time to list out three talking points. You could say, remove these things from your diet, add these few things to your diet, and add these simple activities to your day to lose 20 pounds in a month. You aren't holding anything back. You aren't doing anything silly like, "Explain the WHAT but leave out the HOW." Or even better, "Useful but incomplete." (These are two common, but WRONG, sayings in the information marketing industry.)

Someone could realistically try that advice and it would work provided they stick to it and they complete the gaps. But there are GAPS.

Let's say you had more time. You actually had a full 45 minutes to explain it. That sounds like a lot of time to fill at first, until you develop your idea – then it becomes a matter of trying to fit it in!

If you're teaching weight loss then I hope you have a case study. If the case study isn't someone you've coached then it's you. How did you go from 200 pounds to 180 pounds in a month? Or 150 to 130? Or 220 to 200?

Weight Loss Case Study

For this 45-minute presentation, you focus on the first 1 to 7 days. First, what lifestyle habits need breaking? Is there salt, sugar, and fat addiction at play? What trouble foods do you need to throw out? What ingredients do you need to buy from the store at once or from Amazon.com? What about mindset problems to stick to it? Time management to add meal preparation to your schedule? What about exercise for that added boost?

Could you throw together a list of 10 unbreakable rules that someone HAD to follow to lose 20 pounds in 30 days? And even if they messed everything else up, if they followed those 10 rules, they would succeed?

Weight loss is a good example because there's a clear before and after, it's hugely competitive, and there are plenty of opportunities for not just training but equipment, supplements, recipes, workout programs. One of our students (Dr. Debra Tibbitts) distributed a few products about how to lose weight by drinking these things called "Green Smoothies." She didn't invent them, but you basically mix a bag of spinach, a banana, and coconut water and boom. Stick to that for three meals a day for a few days and you can lose a few pounds easily.

Don't misunderstand me. I'm not giving weight loss advice because that's not my area. I'm also not a vegan, gluten-free, organic health nut – no offense if you are. I'm also in the middle of a 5-day juice "cleanse" as I write this. For $50 a day they ship you six 16-ounce plastic bottles of various juices they've freshly mixed (in Austin, Texas), they pack it in a special box and mail it to you with overnight shipping.

Daily, the juice bottles are to be consumed in this exact order roughly 2-1/2 hours apart:

1. Apple, cucumber, celery, kale, spinach, lemon and parsley
2. Same as above but with ginger
3. Beet, carrot, spinach, apple, lemon, ginger
4. Lemonade, agave nectar, cayenne pepper
5. Apple & cucumber juice again (from #1)
6. Cashew milk with vanilla bean, agave nectar, cinnamon, coconut oil and sea salt

Why am I going off on such a tangent about this juice cleanse thing? Because not only can these people make the juice and ship it for me (and I'm willing to pay $50 a day for what is probably just $10 of actual produce, although I own a juicer and use it sometimes) and it's THEIR SYSTEM. They could probably sell this system, the exact meal plan, as a print book or an e-book and not lose any money. They would probably INCREASE their business because they now have a MESSAGE they can publish, present on guest webinars, guest blog posts, things like that.

That first 45 minutes, focus on the first 7 days, talk about lifestyle changes, this and that and even this sequenced juice cleanse idea. This is what we call a FREE PITCH WEBINAR, which we can discuss later.

The "big picture" for 45 minutes, you'll talk about what someone needs to do in the first 1-7 days of their weight loss journey, then sell a course or book detailing a 30 day plan to lose that weight. All of days 1-30, in the simplest format possible, but with enough information that they don't screw it up or find a way to outsmart your system.

30 Day Plan (In Any Niche)

This idea of a 30 day plan is powerful. Everyone else is trying to carefully add things in or take things out of their free and paid material, or create the encyclopedia of all possible methods of losing weight, while your position is ... that method is excellent if you want to lose some weight and gain MORE back. This other one is okay if you have 6 months or longer to wait. This other technique, you won't even finish the system. But MY plan will take you where you need to go in 30 days.

Once this 30-day plan comes together, you can split it into 4 sections and each section will represent 1 week in the 30 day process. The first week you'll probably have plenty of quick fixes to start them, the final week will have things in place to ensure they keep losing weight and keep the weight off. Week 2 will probably have some huge exciting result and week 3 will contain some crucial element that wouldn't excite people on their own, but needs to be done.

This is how I plan my courses and books. Sometimes these 30 day plans take on a life of their own but that's the logical starting point. What can people achieve in 30 days?

For our podcasting course (PodcastCrusher.com): set up and publish to iTunes, create a second episode with artwork and stock music, then marketing and traffic, and finally monetize that podcast.

Our webinar course (WebinarCrusher.com): Create a 20-minute webinar reviewing someone else's product the first week, then during week 2 launch a product using a free 60-minute webinar session, for week 3 motivate your 4-module course off the ground, and for week 4 obtain consistent traffic and income with a webinar coaching program.

The book-writing course we sell (MakeAProduct.com): structure your book and create the cover in module 1, speak the book out in module 2 and hire a transcriptionist, hire someone to edit the transcript during week 3 after it comes back, and in the final module, upload it to Kindle (for a digital copy) and CreateSpace (for a physical copy), then promote the print and digital books.

I could go on. But the point is this "30 day plan" works in any niche, hardly anyone thinks to do it, yet it's an almost guaranteed way to create exciting content that people will want to buy, start, and finish.

It also puts you in a position of ABUNDANCE. Meaning: you're the one person who knows enough that you have no problem giving away your best stuff (because your paid book or product is even BETTER) while your competitors are careful about the things they reveal.

The "scarcity mindset" versus the "abundance mindset" will come into play for the rest of your life, and it's guided your actions (plus the actions of those around you) whether you realize it.

What do I mean? I mean I was made fun of in school for being smart, maybe you were too. My family made fun of the time I spent on the computer as a teenager and the websites I created. Heck, when I worked at a day job, people made fun of the car I bought. A red 2005 Ford Mustang. It wasn't a super-expensive car ($25,000 or so) but it was flashy (and appropriate for my age of 22 or so) and there were occasional "comments" about it.

I remember one day when I forgot to collect my paycheck at work that month. I wasn't living paycheck to paycheck then, my Internet business paid out far better than that day job (with far less hours) but I still clung to the day job for ridiculous reasons like "safety" and "health insurance." Don't worry, I was young and my main reason for being there was to obtain 3 years of "some" kind of job history on my resume in case the Internet thing didn't work out. I had a plan.

Anyway, I went into the office and picked up my paycheck about 5 days late. Someone in the room made some comment like, "You're going to need that to make your Mustang payments." I didn't become offended, I didn't act better than they, and I just smiled and made some playful comment that I don't remember. No one in that office knew that I paid for that car with cash, all of them thought I'd financed it and could barely afford it.

I'm not going to say something judgmental like, my co-workers made comments to make me uncomfortable, but people will bring you down if you let them. I could have looked at that job like this: I'm stuck here for three years, this isn't worth my time, no one as young as I works here, I'm too good for it, blah blah blah ...

But, instead, those were three good years. They trained me free (gave me technical books to read and sent me to weeklong training centers), they still paid me (I probably would have worked there free), it let me explore my options and it gave me a room to grow.

There's definitely something to be said about "paying your dues" without it as an excuse to be mediocre, or to let your situation bum you out, or to design a life you hate.

I think about the name I used to go by in high school and early college (plus my childhood leading up to that) ... "Bobby Plank" instead of Robert Plank. I used to think about surviving, making just enough money, keeping to myself, being shy, not being hungry for anything else. I'm glad that at some point during college, I learned that I deserved more, without becoming an arrogant ass (another trap many people fall into).

Here's how I thought and acted before "The Transition" ...

- Collector mentality
- Cognitive dissonance
- Reticular activation system
- Limiting beliefs (like too much money is a bad thing)
- Low ticket "dime sale" seller

And after "The Transition" ...

- Full-time entrepreneur abundance mindset
- Failures are just "setbacks"
- Selective ignorance (simplify it)
- Self-motivation (reason)
- Four daily tasks
- "Competitors" just show you how to improve your products

A bonus to switching your beliefs: you'll quickly begin to identify those with the "employee mindset" and phase them out of your life, or at least budget your time with them ... and spend more time with the winners, the entrepreneurs, or at least those who actually support this new lifestyle you're creating for yourself.

Chapter 8: Entrepreneur Mindset

"If your goal is to be comfortable, chances are you'll never get rich. But if your goal is to be rich, chances are you'll end up mighty comfortable."
– T. Harv Eker

The point is that not only have I gone through quite a transformation on the inside, but most successful people I know had a "wrong" way of thinking and had to course-correct somehow.

When hear about things like self-help, personal development, or life hacking, I think, "Why does that concern me? I'm just a coach. I'm just a computer programmer. I'm just a person who sets up websites."

I realized that there were many times, probably daily, when I need that kind of stuff. When I sit in front of the computer, when I can't become motivated, I can't make myself do it, to finish it, and to have fun doing it. I goof around on Facebook and on Twitter, open my e-mail, check my phone, and it's time to turn off the computer and hit that reset button.

Inner Game & Outer Game

I'm going to be sharing with you many techniques that I use when I want to become excited about what I'm doing, finish what I'm doing, and keep doing it repeatedly. Because there's this thing, basically, this is called an inner game and there is outer game, right?

Let's call inner game from all the things about yourself where you're being self-aware, you're being accountable to someone else who's looking over your shoulder, you're running a countdown timer, you're staying on track, you're focused, you're energized, and you know what you're doing isn't working. And when it comes time to shift your attitude, shift your mindset then focus on something else and do something different. That's your inner game.

Then you have outer game, which is actually what is your output, right? Your marketing, your advertising, your copywriting, your traffic, your products, your e-mails – those kinds of things. You can't have one without the other. That would also go as far as to say, if you'll let me say something outrageous, is that I would say that your inner game is about 80% of what matters and your outer game is about 20% of what matters.

Let's think about people who win the lottery. The typical person who wins a lottery loses all that money over the next few years, or they end dead or in a lot of debt, overweight, broke, with no friends, or all the above.

You've heard about people who are famous or successful. You hear about people like Bill Gates, Steve Jobs, Michael Jordan, even controversial ones such as Donald Trump. They didn't reach where they are by accident or by luck. It didn't happen in a straight line.

The Problem with Memorizing, Incantations, Affirmations

Many of them went up, then went down, and then back up again. You can find all kinds of self-help books and discover all these stories about with the guy who invented KFC who heard the word "no" 1,007 times. When Thomas Edison invented the lightbulb, he tried 10,000 ways that didn't work before he found the one that did work. You hear a lot about that and that's where a lot of the self-help stuff receives a bad name.

None of these mindset ideas is "real." It's all based on what we do, and we devise these terms, these analogies, these ways of visualizing what helps us and hurts us. You have people who "over-study."

They were in a bad place at one point. They couldn't complete things, they procrastinated, they were unhappy, and they clung to some saying that worked for them. They might have read a good book that still is relevant called Think and Grow Rich. They might have heard, I don't even know how it goes, but it's, "If you can dream it, you can achieve it."

They say this daily all the time. It worked at first, but overtime, it gradually stopped working and they finished by focusing on the words and they didn't actually put it into action.

I find people all the time where they're well-read. They know all the tips, all the tricks, all the facts, and all the quotes and sayings. If I give them a piece of advice, they'll say, "Oh yeah! What you said, that reminds me of this one thing that Napoleon Hill said, or this one thing that Zig Ziglar said, or this one thing that Jim Rohn or Tony Robbins said." I'm thinking, "That's great. You know the words, but have you actually put them into action?"

That's one thing that I want to be mindful of today. I could have easily talked to you about a hundred various tips for productivity and time management and rattle them off to you one after another. You could have taken plenty of notes and said, "Okay. That sounds good. I agree with that," but I would rather focus on the simple things that actually work. It worked for me for years and hasn't stopped working that you can start using repeatedly because there are two pieces: mindset and productivity.

Fixing Your Attitude

Your mindset is your attitude. The way that you look at life, and your attitude and the attitude of others is contagious. That means that if you hang around with a group of grumpy people all day, you too are going to become a grumpy person.

This became super-clear to me when Lance and I, a few years ago, launched product called Backup Creator. It's a WordPress backup plugin, whether you have or you don't, that's fine. At the time we're recording this, it is now in use on 50,000 sites.

You sell that many copies of one plugin, any piece of software, or any product, and you're going to receive a lot of customer support, which, of course, equals so many people are yelling at you daily and you have a way to deal with that, right? The obvious way is to build a thick skin because it's tempting. Probably, your first instinct is to become annoyed at every complaint, or someone who comes in yelling at you, or someone who, on a rare occasion that we have a refund, take it so personally.

Maybe they yell at you and you yell back, or you become annoyed, or you start complaining and bitching about them all day. It's sad when five-minute or even a one-minute encounter ends by ruining your entire day, but that happens so many times. The reason for that, there are a few reasons, but the way that I see it is that everything we do is driven by the need to gain pleasure and avoid pain. We reach where we have various ways of dealing with obstacles, roadblocks, and pain, and one of those ways is through sympathy or through verbalizing things and talking it out.

In that example, when someone yells at us or maybe they bought and something went wrong with the system, their download link didn't work. They e-mailed us and they yelled at us. When we go and we tell someone else what happens, we feel better, right? That's our seeking of that pleasure.

If that's your response, if that's your defense, if that works for you, then that's fine, but like everything else, it's easy to overdo it. It's easy, if you're yelled at all day, to either dissociate yourself from it and realize, "That's the cost of doing business. We have this low percentage of refund rates." We have these many people talking to us means that we're making this huge number of sales.

It's if people are complaining about taxes. You're complaining about paying so many taxes. You're paying that many taxes because you make even more money coming in yearly.

It's important to use a cliché, have a positive attitude and find the good in everything, because if you don't, if you stay in a mediocre life, if you have this victim mentality, if you enjoyed being beat down, you're not going anywhere. You'll become stagnant, and that will make your life worse and worse. We don't want that.

Chapter 9: Mind State Change

"People often say that motivation doesn't last. Neither does bathing. That's why we recommend it daily." – Zig Ziglar

I want you to be, even this month, 10% more self-aware of what it is you're doing and why it is you're doing it. This is why people become drug addicts, smoke cigarettes, drink alcohol, and exercise. Even things just to move out of whatever state they're in at the moment.

I know that I'm like this all the time. If I am having a bad day, it's good to go out, go for a walk, go for a run, and go to the gym. I used to swim too, go in with one kind of mindset and return out of it. Anytime you go to a movie, because you're sitting there for two hours and given through all this experience, by the time the movie is over, you're a completely different person. Things you were thinking about before are changed. That's important to mix things up, change your state, and break out of these cycles.

If I'm writing, I might have one drink of alcohol. I might have one caffeinated drink to change things, change my state. But like everything else, it can be a tool or it can be something that messes you up.

When we're dealing with these things called time management, at first, I heard about this in college because at least for me, if you're in high school and college, sometimes I would pull what are called "all-nighters." Staying up all night to complete things. Sometimes I would sleep late, stay up late, or wake early and experiment with all the various ways of sleeping and waking.

I used to go to this site called Everything2. I think it's still around but it's basically like Wikipedia, before there was a Wikipedia. I found this thing where it's talking about polyphasic sleep. It's also called circadian rhythms, where, basically, you retrain your brain when you hit the pillow and you lay down, you instantly go to sleep. You instantly go in to REM sleep, what your body actually is sleeping for.

Instead of taking the full eight-hours-a-night of sleep, you sleep in short 15-minute increments, I think, every four hours. That becomes six 15-minute naps per day. You sleep two hours daily and you're awake for the rest of the time. It sounds good but the only problem is that this process ... I lasted about 20 days on this. I couldn't even drive because I was always so exhausted, I was always groggy, and I was always drifting off to sleep.

Apparently, it takes a month or longer to retrain yourself, but even when these people who have retrained themselves, they're at reduced productivity. Now, they have 22 waking hours but they're not always in it. Language skills and language centers are inhibited. Mathematics centers are increasing your brain, but this is one of these things, as an example, called life hacking.

With so many blogs and sites on "life hacking", you can Google these and they will give you top 10 lists. They'll give you these ways of being productive. They'll tell you things like, "For the next seven days, never eat alone. For the next seven days, wear the same five pieces of clothing and cycle through those. In that way you'll save 30 seconds daily so you won't have to put any time or thought into what you're going to wear that day." Or they might say things like, "Here's a blog post on 10 keyword shortcuts."

80/20 Rule

The idea here is that there are various ways to save time that add overtime. I actually have a book on Amazon called <u>100 Time Savers</u>. If you want some of these productivity hacks, you can find them at <u>100timesavers.com</u>. That'll give you a list of little things you need throughout the day to basically save yourself some of time. But that will give you the help you need to make the most out of those days and to keep them up? Because, little tips in things will give you 20% of a boost.

Let's focus on what matters. The 80/20 rule means that 80% of what you do only gives you 20% of the result, and 20% of what you do gives you 80% of the result.

Now, I tell you that and you could do one or two things. You could write that and say, "Oh! That's cool." What it means is that out of all the things you do in your day, only a few things actually matter.

A good example of this is, if you actually – and I'm not telling you to do it because I think it would be a waste of time. I'll tell you what happens. When you sit in your computer, if you categorized, you somehow kept a journal of what it is you did at your computer, you would see this 80/20-rule in play.

You sit it in your computer, maybe you spend a particular time waiting for your computer to start. You spend a particular time checking e-mail, checking Facebook, checking YouTube, and a text comes up in your phone.

A huge chunk of your time can be saved if you treat your computer as a hot seat, as a workstation, and a productivity machine where you have a handful of things to do and that's it, okay? Because, you could spend eight hours of your day and even of your work session at your computer wasting time.

This is why, today, we're talking about the entrepreneur mindset because, what's the alternative for that? It's the employee mindset, right? Someone who has a day job and you've probably been there. I know that I've been there.

When I got paid hourly, that's how it started, and it turned into a yearly salary is, it didn't matter how much I got achieved. I mean, sure I have projects, deadlines, but it didn't matter how much I achieved. I was still paid the same sum.

It was in my best interest to drag my feet. I was not at my peak performance because there was no reward. Doing things faster was no pleasure, and there was no pay for doing things slower to a point. I was in that excellent area that you've probably been in if you're a day-job employee where you're comfortably numb and not completing anything.

When you create your own business whether that's on the side, or you're full-time or you're a partner in business, or what the situation is, you can no longer act like an employee. Because if you do, you'll be running up the clock and you'll ultimately become frustrated.

It might not happen today or tomorrow but you might look back years from now and say, "Shoot! If only I had done four things a day. Those four things were the most important things that I need to be doing and the most profitable activities and I shut out everything else. I removed that other 80%, I would be in such a better place."

Here's what happened is, after discovering The 4-Hour Workweek years ago, I looked into which time management systems are the best to use out there. I found that some were successfully completing things and there's a stack of other various ones. Ones where you have to keep a big long notebook, one where you have to use this piece of software and, of course, they sell it to you, and different things like that.

Many of them were, honestly, too complicated. What I finished by doing was devising the system called 4DT, because if I don't name it something, you're not going to give value to it. It's 4DT, stands for Four Daily Tasks.

Bring this back around to the 80/20 rule, going back to that eight-hour session, the stereotypical eight-hour workday, is it possible that you do 20 different tasks? When checking your e-mail, maybe you check your e-mail five times a day, maybe you check social media a few times a day, and you do everything else, there are probably 20 things you do in a given day.

I don't want to tell you to prioritize or delete the ones that don't work, but out of those 20, would you say that if you had to do four things, that four of them rise to the top. In my case, connecting with joint venture partners, publishing content like blog posts or sending out e-mails, setting up paid advertisements, running webinars – those are all money tasks.

Those are all things that I know make me the most money. But in other things, posting on Twitter, maybe disseminate in article directories. Those are things where I'm probably not going to do them because that's the wasteful 80%. That's helpful.

Accountability & Completion

Remember how I mentioned "Four Daily Tasks" earlier. At once, today, list out what are the four most important things? But I think many people mess up as far as the size of these things because they'll either go too big or too small. They'll say, "Okay, one of my tasks that I need to do is to decide on a title of my blog post." How long would that take you? Two minutes? That's too small a task. We are looking for three tasks, 45 minutes long each, right?

A total of 45 focused minutes with no other distractions going on for us. Then, one of those tasks might be to record a 45-minute video on a subject. One of those tasks might be to create a PowerPoint presentation for a video you might shoot tomorrow. One of those tasks might be to write the entire blog post or write a short version, the first draft, and distribute what it is you have.

You have three tasks that are 45 minutes. "But wait, you asked four daily tasks." What's the fourth task? The fourth task is one task of about 10 minutes. That way, daily, you have one thing that's easy to do, one thing to check off your list. Then three things – I don't want to say they're hard but they're three substantial tasks – and that's it. We don't have to make it any more complicated than that.

Sure, in your previous that you might have thought, you don't have to do all these tiny things. Now, you end grouping them and this will also keep you from shifting your gears and shifting focus to several projects because multitasking does not work. What does work is monotasking, focus. You have these four tasks that you do daily.

Focus = Countdown Timer (Cool Timer)

The next piece, other component to this is that at first, it will be difficult for you to actually put an end cap on things. It's difficult to say, "Okay, this blog post is done. That's it." You use this countdown timer that I told you. This thing called "Cool Timer" and I think there's some equivalent for the Macintosh. I'm not sure but I use this timer.

When I have a task that I know will take me 45 minutes, I set up this timer. There's this thing called Parkinson's Law. It means that if you give yourself eight hours to write a blog post, that blog post will take eight hours to write. If you give yourself only 45 minutes, you'll complete it in 45 minutes.

This timer thing at first, you'll hate yourself. You'll have to retrain your brain, but if you begin completing things before the timers run out, you'll figure out this new system.

Now, once you reach that point, the next step is – it might seem scary but it's not – an accountability partner, which means that you start sharing your four daily tasks list with someone, anyone. If it's a business partner, great, but if it's some random friends, they don't need to know everything you're doing. Show them the list.

What I like to do is, I like to abbreviate project names, video names, and things like that so they don't even have to know what it's about. But they can say at the end of that day, "Did you record a video on this? Did you write a blog post on that?" The answer is yes/no or yes/no.

On a good day, you'll complete all these four things, you're done for the day. You are off the computer and you don't have to worry about anything else.

On some days, you might only finish two or three things. What that means is, let's say you finish three of the tasks. Task number four, whatever reason, maybe you ran out of time, you couldn't work on it, maybe you had other commitments. Tomorrow, you have two things of what you can do.

You can use that task as one of your four tasks for tomorrow or maybe it wasn't important. Maybe it was something such as update the biography on my blog or do some keyword research, it wasn't important, "Fine, I'm not going to do it the next day." Or maybe it was something important, "I've got to make that phone call. I've got to make that video. Okay, that will be the first thing I'd do the next day."

What's cool about this is, if you end by carrying over a task, two, three, or four days, you're either going to shift or move off the path, right? You're either going to do it or you're going to decide it's not important at all.

You have your timer, you have your accountability partner. Now, you might think, if you're used to using a to-do list, this thing of hundreds of bullet points – and we've all been there. All of us know that guy in our life who has such a long to-do list. He doesn't finish anything. He is smart but can't motivate himself, can't complete things, and has the to-do list of all to-do lists.

It's so organized and categorized that you even have a whiteboard on the wall to list it, even the whiteboard never changed and it's so dang depressing.

To-do lists don't work, but the one thing that does help you for is for some long-term planning, right? It does help know what I will be doing in a month from now, if I have some product launch, or a meeting, or an interview, or a video that needs to be done in a week. How do I handle that? For that, I use a calendar, okay? Not a to-do list but a calendar. I like to use Google Calendar.

If you have what's called a Gmail account that actually is excellent for e-mail because it means that you don't have to have your computer on or open. You can go and take your browser to gmail.com and check your e-mail when it's convenient for you. Preferably, that is not one of your four daily tasks. Maybe it's a reward for finishing your task.

It's not the first thing you do in the morning but you use that Gmail account. When you go log-in to your Gmail account, there's a tab that says calendar and you can schedule things on that calendar. The reason I use this above any calendaring system is that if you do a YouTube search for "How to Sync Google Calendar on to Your Phone," you can do that.

You can schedule something on the Web on Google calendar and shows up on your phone or on your iPad. You can share your calendar with other Google calendar users. If you have a business partner, family member, spouse, children, you can share that with others so it stays organized and it's safely scheduled into next week, you can focus on this week. Based on this week, what are my four tasks for today? And we will forward from there.

It seems simple. I know that for some of you, because it's so simple, you might not be in that right mindset to accept it, but I'm telling you this is how to stay productive. The four daily tasks system, you have three 45-minute tasks and one 10-minute task and you list them out. I actually list them in a private blog of mine, I share it with my accountability partner, I run a countdown timer to complete each task, and I schedule things in the future like meetings and things like that into my Google calendar. I don't have to think that far ahead in the future because the calendar does it for me.

This solved many problems because I only have a particular time to complete things, I have my phone over in the other room. I have e-mail and other distractions safely away because I'm laser-focused at present. That important phone call can wait half an hour or an hour because I need to finish this video, I need to make this article, and I need to make a blog post.

By putting yourself in the right mindset, this will help you keep the momentum because when you see all these things, you feel accomplished. If you set things up right, when you see the money that you make from your affiliate promotions, from selling your products, from running your advertisements, this will be motivation to keep going.

If you're not making money, chances are, it's because you haven't completed things. But if you have completed things, if you distribute a product or if you're advertising and your traffic's not converting or not receiving any traffic, you need to adjust and move forward to that next logical step.

So much of this is having a good attitude toward things. The trick, I think, is not having too good an attitude because all of us know people so obsessed, so enthralled, so well-read with all the self-help trickery they have tricked and hypnotized themselves.

What does that mean? It means that they're in denial, overly optimistic, believe that, "It'll all work out. I've put good thoughts out there. I'm not adding any value to the marketplace. I am not building a list. I don't know what my marketplace needs. I'm not giving them products and services and solutions that help solve their problems but doggone it, I'm so dang happy." There's definitely a balance in there. You don't want to be a total grump ruining everyone else's day, but you also don't want your head in the clouds.

What's funny is thinking of which I mentioned is an old book but it's this book where this guy looked into all these wealthy millionaires. What do all of them share? All of them share several traits. Things as if they're all in their mastermind, they use the power of imagination to help them out, they keep trying various things until they succeed and once things do succeed, they keep them going and they systematize it.

Many self-help, religion, and philosophy ideas all copy each other. Why? Because there's only a particular number of things that actually work and there's various ways of saying them.

When you think about your reason, you realize that as someone who is trying to build their own business and become an entrepreneur, money is important. If you're the kind of person who says, "I don't care about money" or you care about money quite a bit, what you care about is a feeling.

I know many people. They have a message, right? They want to share that with the world. They want everyone to love them. They want to become famous. They want to become significant.

I know even more people who want money but they want money to provide for their family and have stability. Have that certainty, have that peace of mind, and don't have to worry about where is the next paycheck, the next bill is going to come from. That's what motivated me quite a bit as far as breaking out of that rat race, no longer being an employee. It was good to have that consistent steady paycheck, but there was no movement for growth in there.

For so many years, I held myself back. I self-sabotaged without even realizing it. I felt bad when I made a lot of money, and I would slow myself when money came in because I was not self-aware and I didn't realize that I needed to reach those goals.

I wanted a fine car. I wanted an attractive house. I wanted a pleasant relationship. I wanted a friendly family. I wanted the peace of mind to not have to worry about money.

Once I had that tied up now, the pleasure I was moving towards and the pain was my present situation. I didn't fall into that trap of hating everything I was, but I knew that I'm uncomfortable enough to move forward and have a better life. I hope that is the direction you are heading towards as well.

Chapter 10: Pull More Money Out of the Internet

"Twenty years from now, you will be more disappointed by the
things that you didn't do than by the ones you did do."
– Mark Twain

There's always room to improve. Even if you're making gobs and gobs of money, I'm sure I can show you a way to squeeze out an extra six figures this year somewhere without doing too much because it's one of those things where even when we reach the crazy advance sales funnel and all that technical stuff, it's always the basics, it's always the fundamentals that we end by missing, that we can always go back to pull more money out of the Internet. That's what we're going to be talking about today is how to set up your own Internet business on autopilot.

What does that mean? For me, that means that daily I wake, money came in overnight. That sounds cheesy but it's true. The reason for that is I have people coming in the door overnight without me doing anything. People coming in the door every holiday, every weekend, all over the world, and what are they doing? They're finding a web page of mine, and usually it's a piece of software or it's a training course. Like, I run several training courses with my business partner, Lance Tamashiro. People are looking around the Internet for some solution to their problem.

What kind of solution? We have, for example, a plug-in called Backup Creator. That plug-in takes someone's website, someone's WordPress blog and makes a backup of it and allows someone to restore it elsewhere and basically clone or copy their website. We have a training course called Membership Cube and what that does is it's a training course where someone can set up their own membership site and host their own downloads, videos, reports, information products, and charge for those. We have a training course called Webinar Crusher, which shows people how to create their online show. Yes, you're listening to an online show, but we're talking about the online show where they can show their screen.

People can hear your voice. You can have hundreds or thousands of attendees show up and listen and watch your screen live and at the end of that one-hour pitch, you can actually have something for sale. All these things are solutions to people's problems. That is what making money on the Internet is all about. Every website that makes money is delivering a solution to someone's problem. One of my favorite websites in the world is called Amazon.com. Maybe you've heard of it. But they're one of the most successful websites. I'm sure I could find all kinds of fancy impressive statistics about it. But the thing about the site called Amazon.com is that they have all kinds of stuff for sale right?

Let's think about this for one second. When you buy something on Amazon.com, why do you buy something there that you don't buy elsewhere? It depends what you're buying. That's a problem. If you're buying, for example, an e-book, a Kindle book, you're buying from Amazon because you don't want to go to the store. You know that all the reviews are there. Maybe Amazon.com sent you an e-mail saying, "Based on your past purchase history, you want to buy this Kindle book. Maybe you were buying something else completely, then Amazon said, "You know what, people who bought this also bought this Kindle book." But either you finished on this site called Amazon.com and based on something on that web page, they convince you to buy.

Maybe you visited a web page and you were going to buy anyway. Maybe you were looking for a particular item, and because that item was cheaper on Amazon, that's what got you to buy it. I know that I sometimes buy things on Amazon.com and pay more money online than in the real world. I'll buy just because of the convenience because I know that my purchase is just one log in a way. I can just click a button and it will show up. It's guaranteed to show up. I trust them. I've done business with them before. Any site that you set up is basically a miniature Amazon.com. But, of course, you can't compete with Amazon.com, can you? Because they have a hold on that marketplace, right?

You can't rely compete with the site, for example, like Facebook because they have hundreds of millions or maybe by the time you listen to this, billions of subscribers and you just can't compete. You have to be different. How can you be different? In my case, I sell a WordPress plugin and I have a website, a web page where there's nothing else on the web page other than a video, maybe some text and a place to buy that plugin. People can't go on Amazon.com to buy my WordPress plugin, right?

There's still plenty room on the Internet for everyone to make money if you are providing value. If you're directly copying someone else, you're not providing value, are you? But if you do this thing called information marketing, you sell information products, that's one where no one's going to duplicate you to copy you. What I do, just to make a long story long, is my niche is software trading and I sell software and I teach people about other software.

I've mentioned a few or our programs. I've mentioned Backup Creator, right? That is what's called a WordPress plugin. WordPress is probably the easiest way to set up a website. If you have like a blog, which means that you have basically an online journal, most of those sites are powered by a piece of software called WordPress. WordPress allows you to add things called plugin. For example, if you wanted to add a pop-up box to your WordPress blog, you use a plugin. By the way, I have a plugin for that called Action PopUp. But here's the problem.

There's these cool things called WordPress plugins but people don't even know how to use them. Sure, there are free videos online, on YouTube. People who create the software create the videos, but when you want to use a piece of software for a particular purpose, that opens a new marketplace for you.

Chapter 11: Carve Out Your Niche by Honing Your Skill

"The things that are easy to do are also easy not to do."
— Jim Rohn

I was a computer programmer and I didn't want to remain stuck at some day job where I was a smart person but not paid much or had to work long hours just for a low sum. I realized at a young age that I wanted to be more than a programmer. I didn't want to be just a programmer, as I'm sure whatever brought you to me, whatever brought you to listening to this audio, and you want to be more than what you are.

I'll give you a few examples. One of our students is the story boarder for SpongeBob Squarepants. His name is Sherm Cohen. I'm sure he makes good money. I don't want to ask but he created Spongebob. He draws for "Hey Arnold" and much of other shows. SpongeBob, he does the storyboard and sketches it out, does all the characters, all that kind of stuff. That's great, right? That's great unless you have a boss, except you have the skill. It's always kind of fun to show someone else your skill, isn't it? If you don't know how to set up your web page, if you know how to be right ranked highly in to Google, then that's a fun skill.

Many of our students have all kinds of crazy skills – and they're not always technical. This guy who draws SpongeBob has a class called "Storyboard Secrets." It's a 10 DVD course and he added an online membership component. It's 500 dollars I believe, and he walks through techniques like how to frame a scene, how to add depth and crazy artist concepts I don't understand, but people pay big bucks for that.

What's cool about that business model is, first, it's something that he loves and enjoys doing. To be honest, he probably would have created those videos free. But although he's charging money for them, he did the work, put in the time, put in the effort once, and created that product once. Then, he put those videos online. He sent those DVDs into a fulfillment Center. Then, someone is looking around the Internet and for one reason or another, they're looking for a course on storyboarding.

I'm friends with him on Google+ and on Facebook. Whenever he posts anything, he receives tons of responses and many of these responses come from other big name artist, other cartoonists. When I say other cartoonists, I mean people who have cartoons on TV or who draw movies like digital animators even. He has this huge following of people who, for one reason nor another, want to become successful a story boarder, who want to know how to refine their skill, how to know the advanced techniques, how to put together a portfolio so they can be hired, basically everything art school failed to teach them, or maybe art school taught them but now that's outdated or they could have learned a few extra techniques or maybe they can't afford art school at the moment but they still want to move ahead.

Either way, they look at this web page. They find the web page. They search on Google. They go on Facebook. However, they find this web page, they find it, and they see that he has course called "Storyboard Secrets." They see the bullet points and all the modules and for some reason they say, "I want that."

Then he says it's $500. For some people, $500 is expensive. For some people, $500 is cheap because it's cheaper than the $120,000 who would cost to go the San Francisco Academy of Art School. For some people, they say $500 is an investment in my future. Whatever they're justification is, then they can click a button. They can pay money right there online, then they download the videos and watch the videos online, then their disks are sent to them in a few days.

But the point is that it kind of happens on autopilot. People who don't make money online, they're missing one of the several pieces. I shouldn't say several. They're missing one of the pieces till they start online and there aren't that many, okay? If I can just take out a piece of paper and I just write a couple, because I kind of want to talk to you immediately. They need a niche.

A niche is like what we just talked about, storyboarding. Another of our students, his name is John Braun. He's the "Hitman Advertising" guy and his niche is carpet cleaning. Again, a goofy topic, right? I think he has like natural carpet cleaning business. I'm not sure if he still goes in to people's homes. What I mean, whenever someone buys a new home or for they just want to fix their home, they attract a team of people who come in and deep shampoo the carpets or remove all the stains. He wanted to improve his carpet cleaning business and realize that by using things like building an e-mail list, by caring about where he was ranked in Google, by setting up a Facebook fan page worrying about social media, he can achieve a heck of a lot more business and he can show the system to carpet cleaners in other areas.

The "Competitor" Myth

What's cool about this is not his competitors because when you have an off-line business, you can only reach a particular area, right? You can only take your carpet cleaning equipment an hour or two drive away. Maybe not even that far. If there's a carpet cleaner countrywide and their business is struggling and he just enjoys teaching this, now he can become the authority, the expert, whatever buzz you want to call it about improving a carpet cleaning business.

We have a chiropractor in Australia who bought <u>Backup Creator</u> and what he does is he set up his website in a particular way. I think he set up his chiropractor website with a particular color scheme and he uses WordPress and he has certain ways of showing direction to the business, the business address, maybe even a way to book in the appointment, but he has this whole system. This chiropractor on Australia, he sales websites, pre-made websites, for thousands of dollars to other chiropractors because he has the skill, I'm sure. He can fix your back, but he can show other chiropractors how to improve their business.

I could just go on and on. We have a student, Bob Molton who teaches guitar. He says, "You could go to the music store. You could find some guitar instructor on Craigslist, pay him hundreds of dollars, go to his house, spend all this extra time, work around his schedule, or learn the guitar online at your convenience from me and you receive all that extra stuff."

You have this thing called a niche, right? Even if you think about Amazon.com, their niche is broad but even if you think about it, are there things that you cannot buy on Amazon? On Amazon, their niche for a long time was books, right? Then, you could also buy DVDs, electronics, now digital books. To make it simple, Amazon's niche is physical products. If we can ignore that e-books, the Kindle stuff just to make it simple, Amazon's niche is physical products.

You need a tight niche just as Sherm has storyboarding, John Braun has carpet cleaning, and Bob Molton has teaching guitar. When I began marketing online more than ten years ago (or maybe even longer because you might listen to this later), I thought, "I don't know anything about the Internet but I'm going to teach people how to make money online." That doesn't work.

Here's what I know: this thing called computer programming, this thing called PHP programming, and years later it also became WordPress plugins.

But I thought, "I have the skill and what I need to do is to be paid for it." I was paid a few hundred dollars to set up someone's website. It was cool because I was 16 and I was paid $300 to set up someone's website with three columns and a few pages but I think it was like 5 pages for 300 dollars. It took me all weekend, but at that age, 300 dollars? I mean, I had friends who worked all summer just to receive 300 dollars, which was awesome.

Chapter 12: Make Money by Solving Desperate Problems

"If you have not yet achieved greatness in your life, it is because you have been willing to settle for less."
— Napoleon Hill

That turned into networking on forums. These days we have LinkedIn, Facebook, twitter, Google+, we have social media sites, but it's the same idea. We still have forums as well. It's even easier now to find the right person. I network and I went on these various message boards to become hired. I posted on programming boards and usually on those message boards, discussions forums, I came across people who kind of said, "Help me with my computer homework. Help me fix this plugin, this piece of software. That didn't help me." But what I stumbled on, I found a few other message boards like SitePoint, DigitalPoint, and Warrior Forum and these gad people who were setting up websites, and many of these websites were actually making money.

Imagine that, going where the money is and that lead to people who had a demand, a need for a programmer. They need a programmer to code something up. One of my big breaks, what happened was I met someone Theresa King. I don't want to tell you my life story. I'm not one of those things but this is just trying to help you. I met someone named Teresa King who wanted a PHP script or plugin made that would protect online payments. Back then, early 2000s we didn't have this technology.

Back in the day, you could right click and view the source code of a web page and find a way to obtain products without paying. Kind of scary. Teresa wanted protection against that, a payment redirector. Someone would pay her money, and that buyer would be sent to a web page. They could download a report or piece of software, but if they didn't pay money, they were locked out.

We created a plugin that solved the need the protected digital products. Because if we sold this thing for $50 and someone look at it and said, "That costs 50 dollars but that's going to save me 500, 50,000 dollars down the line, it's worth that 50 dollars. It's a useful tool." Later, I would earn bigger and bigger amounts and take on bigger and bigger projects.

Someone would say, "I have a problem. I need you to code this program for me. I'm going to pay you money." That went on and on and on, then I got to where I wanted some leverage. I was basically an employee. The whole time I was trying to avoid becoming an employee and I turned into the thing I was avoiding. Instead of having one boss, I was a temporary worker. I will just go from boss to boss weekly depending on who hired me on the Internet that week. Something had to change. What I did was I created an information products.

This means that I noticed the patterns. I noticed that when I was hired repeatedly for these various tasks that people kept asking for kind of the same stuff. People would ask for what's called an e-mail autoresponder. They'd want a program that sends out e-mails to people who ask for a free product. People who willingly enter their e-mail address. People would ask for pop-up boxes. People would ask for quiz script. Maybe they could sell a product or sell access to membership site and inside that, have someone take a test to prove they understand something.

If you would ask me these things repeatedly, just as if I'm sure Bob Molton, the guitar instructor, would find himself teaching the same lessons to a beginner guitar player, the same kind of lessons to an intermediate guitar player, teach how to read music, how to do rhythm, how to do the different finger positions, whatever else there is about learning a guitar, I have no idea, but he finished by going to the same process. But it was important to be paid for this because first, you have to pay the bills. Second, your time is worth something, and finally third, you perfect your own unique formula, your own unique system.

The way that or the kind of programs, plugins, scripts that I would create, it differed from what everyone else created, right? Whatever it is that you do. If you're a writer, your writing process differs from everyone else's. You weren't just a writer, are you? You're a copywriter, article writer, ghostwriter, something like that, or like a blogger. You have your own little unique niche. Within that, you have your own unique way of doing things.

At first I tried to teach programming but my crowd didn't want that. Because again, where is the money at? Was the money at teaching programming? It kind of wasn't. I wasn't going for the nerds because the nerds didn't have money. I was going for the business owners, the marketers, and what they wanted were plugin play solutions. They wanted to just pay me and have me do the work for them but I say, "What if I give you the next-best thing for 1% of the cost?" What I would do is I took about seven of my most asked PHP solutions, software plugins and put them onto one package.

I would say once you use all seven of these and you could use these seven in any order, use just one, use them all, but this will all achieve a particular purpose and that purpose is you put on your website and you make more money. I finished by selling so many of these products, right? Probably my favorite one, looking back in the day, was called sales page tactics. These were different sites. I think one has 19 scripts, 19 plugins. Everything is like you could put in an account on timer. Here you go. Here's the code. Copy and paste it. Boom, it's done and I would even throw an extra instruction on, for example, how to adjust to do what you want.

I'd say, "Here's a countdown timer." If you want a giant countdown timer, change this, this, this and this. One point I was looking, what makes me unique? Why should someone buy from me instead of some other copycat and at this point, there are copycats, but if you stick with me on this audio, you're going to figure out why copycats don't matter.

Are there other story boarders beside Sherm Cohen? Yeah. Are there other carpet cleaners besides John Braun? Yes. Are there other guitar instructors besides Bob Molton? Heck, yes. Why buy from them? Why buy from me? Why buy from you? That answer depends on the person.

From Service Provider to Product Creator

My answer at first was that these are scripts that I actually use, because when you go to other programmers to learn programming, at the time, if you go to a bookstore to find a book on programming, what do you find? You usually finish with a five-hundred or six-hundred page encyclopedia that tries to teach every little thing and it makes sure to just cram all kinds of knowledge you don't need just to fill space because if they have a massive book on computers, then it's in their best interest to give you the giant book sitting next to the small book, right?

One thing I would say is that this isn't for everyone. If you're a nerd looking to program, you don't want this. But again if you're a marketer, a business owner who wants to increase your convergence to make money, then yes, use these plugins. Aside from that, the other thing is that I like the mid-2000s. I discovered how to record the video.

Now you might be able to tell from the way that I speak I'm not a professional speaker. I'm a lot like you. I was nervous at first about being on camera, being on the microphone, someone hearing my voice and I avoided it. But mid 2000s I started recording videos just because making a product took too freaking long. I'd have to code stuff, write stuff, and it wasn't worth all that time. I start recording these things on video.

I had plenty of ideas because I had plenty of people wanting to hire me and I got to where I said, "You know, you could hire me but how about I just make this for you free? I'll make new products with this as one of the seven plug-ins. It will come out next week. You'll receive it free and I'll put your name in my book and I'll explain this exact message. You can copy and paste this exact e-mail you just sent me and asked me for this problem to be solved. You e-mail me asking me, can you put a countdown timer on a web page? You asked, can you set up a web page so when someone first visits that page, they see this message.

When they return a second time the message changes to that. If someone comes back a third time, the message changes again. When you asked me, can you set up a plugin where it shows one thing on a web page then by Friday the price doubles or by Saturday, the offer is gone.

Instead of taking money once for that, I would take the idea, give them credit, put it in my product and make a lot more money by selling to many people, right? Before, I was paid, say, 500 dollars, a thousand dollars, but now I put this into a $20 information product and sold a couple hundred copies and now made 2,000, 3,000, 5,000 dollars. It just got ridiculous and I keep doing it. I keep doing it where I would launch two products a week, okay?

A product met that I've recorded about maybe 90 minutes a video make about seven plugins and have probably a 50-page report explaining what's in it. I would write a web page, we call this a sales letter, where I would explain what was in the product. I would set up what's called the payment button, which turns up when we take orders automatically and it downloads a page where someone could download a product.

I would send out an e-mail to my subscriber list telling to all that I have this new product. Most of my list at that time for people who bought previous products, then I would go out and promote this product on other message board. This was building a business. Then I mistakenly thought of it as a hobby. I thought okay, I'm in college. I'm reaching the end of college. I'm looking for like an internship of a job and this is an extra money on the side. Because I had that mentality, I thought twice about spending more than a few hours on it. Those hours I did spend were not focused. I know that you've been there, right?

You've been there to where maybe you spend all day on Twitter, all day checking e-mails, all day buying this, buying that, buy this $5 product, this $1 product, this $50 product. Buying, buying, buying, and not making any progress. I was treating it like a hobby not as a business yet but I wanted money. I find a way to make some easy money and I was also worried that if I sat around for too long that this system wouldn't work anymore.

That Internet marketing would change. The Internet marketing kind has change. The basics still work but things change over time even from one year to the next. I was worried about competitors, so I made sure to distribute two products a day. What happened is I would come home from class, then at one point, I reached where I also had a job in the university. I would come home a day of classes and working. I would have my products ready to go from a couple days before. Usually I would put most of the effort into this like during weekends, then during the week release, all right?

I would come home. I would upload everything. Have everything ready to go. I would send out an e-mail. I would be ready to go to the gym and become all settled, eat dinner and check back on my computer before I left for the gym and have a thousand dollars sitting in my PayPal account, what we use to receive payments. A thousand dollars that I didn't have an hour before that had just poured in. Cool stuff. I had to go out and go to the gym. I had a couple of gym buddies people where all of us had an agreement to meet at the set time and a set location and kind of exercise.

I do that, then return after about an hour or so maybe we'd hang out and but I'd return a few hours later at night and have another $1,000 in PayPal. Then, it would stop. I don't want to tell you that, "I became a millionaire overnight." But that was some appealing spending money. It took a lot of the pressure off because I living paycheck to paycheck. I had several sources of income. I had this job. I only take that job seriously because the sum I made was a few hundred dollars per month, then the income I have from my business was thousands and thousands of dollars per month. Real disparity there. Then, I don't want to tell you my life story, but that's where one of those things had to win and I finished by quitting my job to do this full time and I've been at this time for years and years.

The basic formula hasn't changed but what has changed is that instead of creating new products every time instead of thinking, "What new thing am I going to create?" many times, I'll just promote something that I already have. But the components, and many marketers will tell you this, the components that breaks it down to is this thing called the list, this thing called traffic, and this thing called offers. If you think about even my favorite website, Amazon.com, they have a list, they have traffic, and they have offers. If you do a Google search the latest camera, even something like Apple iPad, on the front page you're almost guaranteed to find search result from Amazon.com.

That's their traffic, right? Amazon has this thing called an affiliate program where others can create blogs, videos, link to other products, and receive a commission. That's their traffic, right? Offers are simple because they sell all kinds of those other offers, right? They sell Kindle books, physical books, electronics, and all kinds of office supplies crazy stuff. I've bought meats off Amazon.com and it comes packed in dry ice. It's like healthful corn-fed beef or something. But that's from Amazon.com.

You can buy a list of weird things in Amazon.com but they have all kinds of offers. Streaming videos, music, just all kinds of stuff, right? Then, this final component, which you probably didn't even realize is they have the most valuable piece of all this is a list.

List Building & E-mail Marketing

Now, what's a list? A list is they have a list of customers, list of prospects. If Amazon.com wants more money, they contact this list. You might be thinking, "Well, that's not true. Amazon doesn't e-mail me," but they do.

I know they e-mail me weekly. Every week, an e-mail comes in from Amazon.com and usually it'll be like a graphic e-mail and they'll say, "Look, our latest DVD releases. Look at our latest computer parts or latest laptops." I'm so used to receiving this e-mail that I don't even think twice about it. Many times, I'll click over and by something I don't even need or something that I have needed, but Amazon is tricky because they track things that you search for or that look at but they didn't end buying it but they'll e-mail you a week later and say, "You were looking at this. Do you want to buy it?" You're like, "Yeah, I forgot. I was going to buy that water filter. I was researching water filters and you sent me this again. I'm now going to buy it." A list is what you want.

A list is traffic on demand. If you think about it as well, if you're on Amazon.com and you see something and you go in to buy it, do they just ask for a credit-card information? That's part of it. But they want you to log in to your Amazon account. Why? Because they're adding you to a list because they want to track you personally. Taking payments is excellent, but taking repeat payments is even better. When I say repeat payments that might be a monthly fee because, for example, if you buy like toilet paper or many of their grocery items, you can actually set it up for them to ship you more of that every month or every few months. It's kind of cool. That's one thing.

But in addition, if you just buy one thing and a few weeks later they send you another e-mail and you buy that, that's still recurring income on their part, right? To have a successful Internet business, you have to have a list, you have to have traffic, you have to have offers.

One Foot on the Brake: Why Slow?

At one point in my early online career, I figured out a way to make $2,000, not wad of money but $2,000 and I could have easily made $2,000 once, then not done it anymore. Maybe will do that.

They have this thing that's called going around with your life with one foot on the gas, one foot on the break. Their goals is just to make a thousand dollars online, just make $10,000 online. They reach it and they quit and they're out of it forever. I don't want that for you. I want you to receive everything you've always wanted and to keep pushing yourself and move out of your comfort zone and not overwork yourself, not burn yourself out, but move things forward along as fast and as far as you can make it.

The way I always think about it is what if I look back and I'm 100 and I think, what if I could look at the present from the future, if that makes sense, and there's more that I could have done? I always kind of try to have or not try but they have that mindset in minds, but that sounds kind of money, but that's what I'm always thinking about is I want to shortcut, I want do as much as possible, which means that if I'm going to send out one extra e-mail, then I'll do it. If I have to contact one extra person and make one extra product, take this seriously, treat it is a real business, then I will.

That's what I want to tell you today, is why slow if you can figure out how to send an e-mail and make some money from that? Then why not send 10 e-mails? If you can make money from one product, why not create 10 products? That's the thought of the day today, is why slow? The answer to that question is, there's no reason to slow. Find something that works, repeat it, keep using it until it doesn't work, then find something else that does work, if that makes sense.

List + Traffic + Offers = Autopilot Internet Business

Right back at it, we're going to figure out exactly what pieces you need to start an Internet business on autopilot and we send these list, traffic, and offers. What sounds great, but what do you actually have to set up? I've mentioned earlier that we have a course called IncomeMachine.com. In that course, we analyze the various components you need to make money online. I'll list them to you right away and we'll send them. Mention your niche, right? Carpet cleaning. We started wording that kind of stuff.

You need an opt-in page, a web page where people can enter their name and e-mail address. You need an e-mail autoresponder sequence, which means that you built that list but now you have to actually send people messages. You need to tell them what to buy. Now, what you tell them to buy. We need what's called a sales letter, a web page where someone can click a button, pay your money, and receive something. You need a membership site. Well, let's just say membership site/download page.

We need somewhere where someone can get that. Then, let's say that you also need a blog, even if it has just a couple of posts so you're selling based on what you have for sale and that's good, but you also have your personality. That's why I'm making this podcast. That's why you posted it on Facebook, maybe you market it on Facebook, but it's that having a branch but there's also the personality part, so important, and finally you need traffic.

The thing that I listed were niche, opt-in page, e-mail, autoresponder sequence, sales letter, membership site, blog, and traffic. It sounds like a lot but it's basic. Anyone who makes any kind of money online for more than a few months has most of these, if not all, these components set up. You need to choose a niche, choose, say, for example, if you're teaching guitar. Now, based on that, you need to set up what's called an opt-in page and this means that people go to their web page and you say free report, "How to Play These Four Pop Songs On the Guitar in Less Than 30 minutes and Impress All Your Friends."

Now if someone is looking around the Internet and they're just researching, they're trying to figure out the best guitar course, what kind of guitar material should I buy? Should I buy a DVD from Amazon, a book, a Kindle book, go to an instructor, what should I do? They search it on Google and they find your opt-in. Now, to have this kind of web page, what do you need? You need what's called a domain name. You go to a site like Namecheap.com and you find something called a .com name or a domain name.

You end having a site, for example, like guitarplayingsecrets.com. I guarantee you, that's someone's website. You find a domain name. Having a name is excellent, but now you need a web page. What we do is we also have a thing called a web host. This is much you log in and where you point this domain name. For webhost, we use a service called Hostgator. You find a domain name, you find a web host, and now you just set up a simple white blank opt-in page.

Now, to set up an opt-in page, let me just list one or I guess two final tools. One thing you need is an e-mail autoresponder service, and we recommend a service called Aweber.com where they allow you to collect and send e-mails. Everyone does this. Facebook, Amazon, Apple. The secret to their business is building that list, to have that traffic on demand to set right one message and send it to thousands or millions of subscribers.

You receive an autoresponder service. What they will end doing when you log in to, for example, AWeber, is you create what's called a list, then they give you web form. You copy and paste that web form onto your web page. When you do that and someone sees that you have this report on how to play the guitar. They can enter in their name and their e-mail address, fill that in and you delivered their report by sending them to a download page, but now they are on your subscriber list.

Don't hear me wrong, you're not spamming because what spammers do is they circulate the Internet and they grab e-mail addresses and they find people on their list who didn't ask to be on. But this person voluntarily we call opted in your list and every e-mail you send has what's called an unsubscribe link so anyone who joins, they can leave your list but they're not stuck there. They chose to join because they're a targeted lead to someone who is researching guitar instruction. They come to your site, they see and receive this report with ton of instruction.

They receive their free report, then over time, you can send them e-mails or maybe even in your report, you have links to like a paid product or guitar coaching. If you recommend a particular guitar, you have a link to Amazon.com with what's called your affiliate, your referral link. If someone buys the $500 guitar on Amazon, you receive a commission. You receive a percentage of that. Several ways of monetizing this but it starts because someone is looking around the Internet and they enter in their name and e-mail address to receive this free report.

They read that report and maybe at the end of the report, you send to go back to your sales letter. You mentioned this Amazon.com affiliate links, all this kind of stuff, and maybe the click and view web page and maybe not buy yet then in a week, another e-mail is sent out automatically. They read it. They click over and they buy. You know what? They might never buy. They mind decide that they're not in the guitar instruction. They might buy it from someone else. But it's a number's game!

Many people on my e-mail list is like 2004, then years later in 2012 or even further down the future, they end buying at that point years and years later. It doesn't matter if one person finds you and doesn't buy, but you can receive a thousand, ten thousand or more people on to an e-mail list and they're all interested in storyboarding, carpet cleaning, guitar instruction, WordPress plugins, then chances are that many of those will buy and once you're involved in Internet marketing or if you're already in it, once you split test or shock your links, every number is low.

If you have a sales letter that converts that at 1%, you're doing excellently. If you send out an e-mail to your subscribers and 1% of your whole subscriber base clicks over from one e-mail, you're doing well. We need large numbers just to make a living on the Internet but we have to have a list, traffic, offers, choose a niche that have an opt in page, we can start building that list, then we send out e-mails, send out an e-mail autoresponder sequence that people will eventually buy.

Affiliate Marketing Explained

What will they buy? We can send them to Amazon.com. That's an easy one. The good thing about Amazon.com is they sell everything. There's probably something that you can recommend. We have students into weight loss, dieting, exercise, so they can link to protein bars on Amazon.com. Maybe we can have them on the auto-ship as one of those monthly things. They can link to $500 Vitamix blenders. They can link to other people's video courses and receive a commission. The problem is that it's low commission. I believe it 15% if they link directly to something, 5% for the next three days if someone clicks, then buys a different item. Low percentage.

Luckily, there's a site called Clickbank where they have the whole marketplace and some of these various vendors will sell products and give away 50% to 75% commission. Someone might have a product on ClickBank about how to achieve rock hard apps. I forget what it's called. It's called something similar to that. I think it's like 100 dollars and they give away 75% commission, so you make a $75 sale. If someone has a product on ClickBank on how to improve your memory for $20 and they give away half that, you receive $10 per sale.

If you can receive a $1000 sale, that's a pleasant little commission. With this thing called affiliate programs on the Internet, affiliate marketplaces and people will list them because they need people like you to send them traffic, and for that traffic you send them, you receive a commission, right? That's good to start. In Income Machine, we lead you through all this kind of stuff, then we say, at some point, you're going to want to go to the next level. You're not going to want to slow.

You going to want to keep it going and keep ramping up, keep expanding. Recommending on people's products are excellent but at some point you're going to want to teach your own stuff like how at first I provided a service and that was fine until I notice that everyone else did a crappy job of teaching programming and they were teaching to the wrong crowd. They were saying, "Here's how to create what's called a hello world. Here's how to make your first computer program," and I was thinking, "No. Don't learn all of it. I'm going to give you the basics and put in on the web page."

You're going with some point through boredom or frustration or just plain old being hungry. You're going to think of your own information products. That's where all the cool stuff happens. We use a tool called Camtasia Recorder. It's 300 dollars. It's got a 30-day trial and you can show your screen, show a PowerPoint, show your browser, show a piece of software, talk, talk, talk, record it, and now you have a video.

Product Creation

Even a one-hour video is something you can sell. Even a one-hour CD is something you can sell. We create what's called a sales letter.

Someone's going to come to your web page and something you'll say will convince them to buy. Like how on Amazon.com, you might not know which book to buy today or which computer to buy, but something on in Amazon web page convinced you to buy, or you came to that page ready to buy and they just showed you the order button.

But either way, you have a web page that has some words on it, maybe a video that explains what you have to offer. Here's how to buy. That's called a sales letter. So far in the steps we've taken, we've decided a niche like carpet cleaning. We've created an opt-in page so when someone is researching carpet cleaning, they find us and we prove to them that we know a lot. We know so much that we're even giving them some information for me. As on this podcast, I'm giving all the steps. The problem with the podcast though is that I can't show you. I can only give you the big picture.

I can only kind of guide you part of the way. You can take notes and try to watch free YouTube videos, read some articles, but you're not going to obtain the complete picture unless you join Income Machine (at IncomeMachine.com). I'm explaining this to you person-to-person, as a friend like you would explain to like a family member or a neighbor or someone I went to school with or an ex co-worker how to do this. That's what you do as well.

Whatever your field is, you explain to someone how to perform a task. What's cool about software is that I can talk all day about how to clone this or how to have that back, because at the end of the day, they need my software to do it. You choose a niche and set up an opt-in page giving away something free like a report.

Now you're building a list, you send the messages. At first, send them affiliate links or other people's offers where you receive a commission, and if you can create your own product, create your own sales letter, great. I wrote my first sales letter when I was 17 or 18, and do you know where it was? It was headline, 10 bullet point, and order button. That web page made me $400 overnight. Once I figured out the traffic part, maybe a thousand dollars over the next several months.

It doesn't have to be fancy. If people are already looking for this, if you have a targeted crowd, if you're creating as product based on the need not just for fun, like most people who create products and books do, then you're going to have an easy time selling. Backup Creator that's used on tens of thousands of sites and I didn't want to create it, but I was continually asked to make it. I notice that the existing solutions weren't that good. I knew I would use this plugin I created in a way that was different from everyone else's, so adding value and now it's selling what people want.

People are already looking for it. People are ready to buy it from you for it. I want to just create and give it to them. That way, you don't have to put a lot of effort in the selling. You don't have to turn someone's whole way of thinking around. They're coming to you. They're searching on Google. They're on YouTube. They're searching on the site who published articles called EzineArticles because they want the solution. You put that in your sales letter. Once someone clicks and buys, you send them to what's called the download page, a hidden web page and there's a link to obtain the report, their video.

The next logical step than this is a membership site. You've probably seen the membership site because you probably logged in to Amazon.com or to Facebook today or to YouTube. These are membership sites, or Gmail. A membership site is the site where someone can be a member. What's interesting is that when you sell, say, like your beginner guitar course in video format, you can send them a DVD. You could put a video on a web page. But if you create a form something someone can complete after they buy where they can become a member, now we're talking because someone can interact to others inside that membership, someone can log back in and see any kind of updates.

When they're ready to buy the intermediate guitar course, the next course, you can put a link to that in the member's area, you're building a list so everyone who buys it from you now receives all in your list as a paid buyer. A membership site is valuable. But you have to put everything in place. You have to crawl before you can run. You have member site. Now, you have the money-making part figured out, right? Niche, opt-in page, autoresponder sequence, sales letters, membership site.

Now, we kind of have to do public relations and that means set up a blog, preferably if "YourName.com" or a variation is available, then grab that. If not, I know people who brand themselves, for example, if there's another Sherm Cohen who owned this name, then he would be Sherm Cohen storyboard. Obtain some variation of "YourName.com" and set up what's called a WordPress blog. Again, at IncomeMachinne.com, we show you all that.

Set up a blog, put your name on it, and now and then, just talk about stuff. If you find something interesting on the Internet, why post it on your Facebook where it's going to be buried and forgotten in a month? Why not put on your blog where people can find it by searching on the Internet and they see and know what you're talking about, then it links back to your opt-in page, it links back to your sales letter for your product.

Many times, I notice that just from looking at my logs and my tracking and all that, people will come to a web page of mine ready to buy, then they'll leave. They'll kind of do a background check on me. They'll look at and they'll say, "I'm about to buy this backup plugin, but let me just search Robert Plank WordPress and let me just see what Robert Plank talks about," and they see that I have hundreds of articles on article sites, hundreds of videos on

YouTube, hundreds and hundreds of blog posts, plenty of blog posts on other people's blogs that I've written for and talking about WordPress technical stuff, marketing, then they say, "Okay, this guy knows what he's talking about."

That's what someone should say about you as well. You have your blog and that's where you should update maybe once a month. Now, we want this thing called traffic, kind of the tricky part. Now, we need people to link back to you and that means set up what's an affiliate program like how Amazon has. This means that may be we'll have to pay for some advertisements on Facebook or on Google, we'll have to distribute some articles and videos, some concept. It's as if we have our paid product and our best stuff is there. Our exact system is there. All our tools and templates, it's there.

It's all "too good to give away" but that it's so good that in comparison, we're fine writing articles or making podcasts, for example, or free videos online with a few pieces of the puzzle just because we enjoy it that much. If we can solve somebody's small problem free and they become a fan of us for life, then we'll end by being rewarded because we build a huge list and where there is something for sale, then they will buy that. I'll just tell you at once, I have a YouTube channel.

If you go to youtube.com/phprobert, now and then, if I have something that doesn't quite fit into a product, then I'll make a video for it. Sure, someone video show you some of my plugins for some of them, for example, I like an hour video on YouTube showing how to set up WordPress multi-site, just a technical thing, but I don't want to sell up product on it. I was messing around with it and I said, "I use this. Let me make a video about it."

You need to build a business that you can be proud of. I can even obtain a small result for someone and show them how to repair a home, how to start a business, how to save money on your taxes, that's something that people will pay money for. There's no point in doing it once, then stopping. I don't think there's a point in slowing or tiring yourself.

You want to wake to a "big pile of money every morning" because people found your website overnight, they were a member of your membership site and they bought overnight. It just happens. Maybe it started slowly but at some point, it turns into an autopilot system because you set up a niche, opt-in page, e-mail autoresponder sequence, a sales letter, membership site, a blog, and had consistent traffic coming in.

I run webinars, I set up membership sites, I sell software, but I believe in systems. You and I are going to have a lot of fun. I'm going to share a lot of cool, secret, and advanced techniques on these episodes that you're going to implement right away.

For example, I can write what's called a "sales letter" in a day. I can complete an e-mail in five minutes, a blog post in 10 minutes. I can sit and in 6 hours today, create a hundred articles and repeat that as many times as I want. Plenty of cool systems, plenty of cool strategies, but don't be distracted by the simplicity of it. Know where the problem is, where you need to focus, and one thing we didn't have time to reach was a thing I have called four daily tasks, which means don't have a long to-do list, let's just have four simple things completed daily.

Part 3: Family & Friends vs. Business
Chapter 13: Aggressive Mediocrity

"If friends disappoint you over and over, that's in large part your own fault. Once someone has shown a tendency to be self-centered, you need to recognize that and take care of yourself; people aren't going to change simply because you want them to."
– Oprah Winfrey

As an entrepreneur, you're taking part in a lifestyle that few people understand (although they want the same rewards you have, don't they?)

Making this whole "working for yourself" thing actually happen requires you to be JUST DISSATISFIED ENOUGH with your current employment to do something about it, but also dedicated enough to follow a few simple rules (like building a list and bringing traffic), although being just barely creative enough to be different in the marketplace and adapt enough when things don't quite go your way.

Too much or too little of those criteria and it won't work out. It's easy to goof off checking your stats, e-mail, forums, goofing around with "projects" and making yourself comfortable with being unemployed – you need something to drive you. But at the same time you don't want that hunger to turn into envy and jealousy ... quite a tall order!

When you're figuring out your business and making money (it might take a few months), you're going to encounter resistance not just from yourself (that negative voice), friends (what the heck are you doing on that Internet thing anyway?) but friends as well.

Basically, you're going to feel like an alien, at least at first, because no one else seems to reach you and the solution for that is to surround yourself with successful people. If you can join a community or a mastermind of people REALLY making money (there are some that only claim to), then you won't have to spend so much of your time and energy explaining what you're doing.

Here's the truth about successful people …

- "Your income is the average of your 5 best friends" – Jim Rohn
- "The best revenge is massive success" – Frank Sinatra
- "You get good at what you do a lot of" – Robert Hunt
- "Rich people make decisions quickly and change them slowly. Poor people make decisions slowly and change them quickly." – Napoleon Hill

What do all these ideas mean when rolled together? It means that successful entrepreneurs all think in a particular way, and it's way different from the typical person. Instead of being petty, saving money, beating others down to make themselves look good, finding people "beneath them" or relying on luck to make it happen … successful people find a way to make it happen.

Here's a term I despise when making your business and your life work together: this idea of "BALANCE." Yuck! "Balance" implies that may be your family life can be at 100%, and your business is at 100%, and maybe if there's time to fit a day job in there (before you go full time), it's 33%-33%-33%.

What a load of crap! Look, one doesn't have to take away from the other. You can have a good year in your business, make a wad of money and take your family on the vacation you've always wanted. Your family can give you the encouragement you needed to put that product out there, run that webinar, or make those extra connections or joint ventures. Many times, Lance and I have worked personal stories into our sales letters and pitches.

I think a better way of putting things is that you need BOUNDARIES separating your family and your business. That means you might have to be in a meeting, or run a live webinar, and be clear with your family that you are unreachable in your office. Likewise, if you are taking a family vacation, your joint venture partners and customers cannot reach you – you're off the clock.

Students and clients have told me that managing their business and their family is a lot like military deployment on a smaller scale, I tend to agree. Especially during those early months when the hours are longer and the income is lower and you're trying to prove yourself, build a list, create a winning offer … you won't always have time for them during that "temporary" transition.

It's all about priorities but ALSO about honesty with yourself and with them. Don't start using your business to escape your family – I've seen it done!

While we're on this topic of awkward transitions, you might lose friends as you lost friends after high school, after college, or after changing careers or increasing your income. There's a thing I can only describe as "aggressive mediocrity" … basically, many people believe that their current lifestyle (which they're currently unhappy with) is only bearable if everyone's just as miserable – if not MORE miserable – than they are.

Don't let them manipulate you. If someone is discouraging or hindering your efforts to reach where you want to go, you have a decision to make. You can quietly and politely cut that person out of your life (there's more fish in the sea) or you can explain to them that you need someone supportive in your life to be happy for you. (And not sarcastically.)

Look, when you're starting your business, there's plenty to worry about:

- Fear your idea isn't **good enough**
- Fear of **competitors** and copycats
- Fear of **government** over-regulation
- Fear of being **sued**, libeled, or blacklisted
- Fear of being **hated** or irrelevant
- Fear of **self-doubt**
- Fear of having a small success and not being able to handle it or **repeat it**

I could go on. But with all that worry in front of you, you don't need friends and family to bring you down BESIDES having to deal with all of that. You NEED them to lift you and make it worthwhile!

Here's something else. The need for free time and introspection. Every successful person I know is smart enough to remove of all the liabilities that stress them out. A stack of debt, overpaid bills, unresolved problems with people, grabs your subconscious and doesn't let go.

If you don't do this already, find 1 hour in your day to THINK. That means go for a run or walk with no cell phone or music player, go for a drive with no one in the car and the radio off, go to the gym or go swimming, have an hour a day to yourself with no voices, no music, no nothing, just your thoughts. Don't even bring a pen and paper to use to write ideas.

Do this for even a few days and you'll find yourself finding peace, finding solutions to difficult problems and thinking more about the "big picture" – specifically where your business and your life is headed.

Later in this book, I'm going to be talking about how my Dad sabotaged himself and sabotaged me as I was growing up. Every computer that I ever owned before I turned 18, he tossed down the stairs. Once, a girl from school called me and he told her I wasn't home. (I was.) Another time, a different girl found out where I lived and showed up asking to see me. He told her I wasn't home. (I was.)

You might be thinking, this Robert Plank guy must have some problems if he keeps fixating on his family problems and about people who sabotage our success.

You're probably right.

But every other successful entrepreneur has similar problems and is using building a business, writing blog posts, creating products to WORK THROUGH and MANAGE their problems instead of hiding them.

I once opened the first few minutes of one of our Product University seminars with the idea that anytime I become angered.

frustrated or enraged with someone else's actions or words, it instantly motivates me to start writing and creating content.

I see someone do or teach the WRONG way to do something, I almost have no choice but to call attention to it, then transition into the RIGHT way to do it.

You're teaching weight loss and everyone else is teaching things that don't work, like take these pills, or "just walk a few minutes a day" or "just drink more water" … and you have a better way, don't ignore that bad advice, use it as a jumping-off point for your writing and marketing.

If your parents were always stressed out about money and took it out on you, have a better handle on your money and your family. If you keep walking past that pile of dirty clothes and it's making you angry, making you angry enough to wash a load or two.

Stress and anger are not always bad in moderation! Especially when it makes you to "clean out the gunk."

Maybe you're a young woman who's been dating a guy for a while who just won't commit, won't marry or won't stop cheating on you, and you become angry enough to finally dump him and move on with your life.

You can use pain and failure as a useful tool to do better, if you so choose. And I feel as if I'm uniquely qualified to impart some of this knowledge to you because I was a computer programmer, I understand systems AND I've been around people with a lot less common sense than I (didn't think that was possible) who knew all the facts but just couldn't implement.

Look, set up a Google Calendar as we've discussed to manage your business meetings and that must-have family time like collecting someone from school or dropping someone else at the dentist. Set up what's called a "Skype Number" so you can give out a phone number that only rings to your computer when you have the Skype program enabled (or the Skype app on your cell phone). Create a "support desk" so if people have pre-sales or technical questions about your business, you can answer them without it overflowing your e-mail and you can eventually hire someone to run that help desk.

If you're so pressed for time at the moment that you can only fit in an hour here and there, make it a point of accomplishing more in those couple hours than most people do all day. Avoid doing things in Degrees of Doneness (you know, "it's 85% complete") and instead complete milestones so you can prove to yourself and your family that you are making consistent progress and that your lives are BETTER now that you have this added freedom.

Don't "shoot yourself in the foot" (or let others shoot you in the foot) and instead REDIRECT your frustration and anger into productivity. You're taking this risk to improve your life and your family and you shouldn't let anyone be in your way ... even yourself!

Chapter 14: Lessons from an Ex Computer Programmer Internet Marketing Geek

"I choose a lazy person to do a hard job.
Because a lazy person will find an easy way to do it."
– Bill Gates

A common question I am asked … out of all the possible things I "could" be doing to make a living online, what actually works? I'll give you a hint: the same things that always worked like building a list, optimizing paid traffic, building relationships and following up with your subscribers, training those subscribers, being in-tune with what your market wants and presenting your irresistible offer in a new and exciting way that gives them what they want and sneaks in what they need!

That's why I want to share what I think are the six most valuable lessons (in both your marketing and your mindset) that have stuck with me over the years that I think will carry you into the next 12 months, then some:

Life Lesson #1: Strategies versus Tactics. You need to know the difference between strategies (things that always work) and tactics (little tricks you have in your back pocket to use now and then). How many times have you heard of a business that relied on one website, or one Google loophole, then one day, poof, it was gone? How many times have you seen a marketer become desperate and discount the price of a product just to pay the bills? Then they were lost on how to pay the bills next month!

Life Lesson #2: Decisions. Every decision you make either changes your actions or changes your mindset. Becoming angry, becoming a victim, "bitching and moaning" are natural ways you're trying to change your mindset but that will lead you down the path of more destructive actions. Instead, turn should-to's into have-to's into want-to's.

Life Lesson #3: Self-Awareness. You don't work as "hard" or as "fast" as you think you do, and you need downtime. You're not an employee in your own business. It's not about running out the clock the same way it is when someone else is paying you for your time. Alcoholics Anonymous has the term, "Progress not perfection." If you want to be paid as little as an hourly employee then act like one, but if you want to be a productive business owner who works smart (not hard) and leverages their time, then do what other successful people do.

Life Lesson #4: Pick Your Battles. You need the ability to fall on my own sword (a little). Apologize when it's necessary and move on when it means you're progressing instead of being weak and surrendering. Bite your tongue and let the other person win if it means more money or more happiness.

Life Lesson #5: Hope for the Best and Plan for the Worst. You need to AUTOMATICALLY backup everything (your desktop and your website), in several locations and in several ways. So many things aren't valuable, or aren't important, until they're gone, and now you'd pay $10,000 for that one missing file that you could have saved by spending 2 minutes clicking a button. You'll grow old someday. You'll die someday. Others around you will die someday. Don't become bogged down by that thought, use it as a tool to focus and reach where you need to go.

Life Lesson #6: Life is too Short, So You Need to Be Everywhere. You're probably thinking too small. You need 100+ articles on the Internet. You need a blog, a podcast, a Kindle and CreateSpace book, a product for sale, a Facebook account, a fan page, a Twitter account, and a forum username on at least a few popular discussion boards in your niche. You need an e-mail newsletter, several opt-in pages, and all these things need to lead right back to YOU.

Chapter 15: Can I Give You 30 Extra Hours Per Month?

"The bad news: There is no key to the universe.
The good news: It was never locked."
– Swami Beyondananda

This is cool. At first it will "seem" like common sense ... then you'll think "that sounds great, but it's not for me" but FINALLY ... once you reach the third step, it'll hit you like a ton of bricks. This has to be the #1 boost to my productivity all year.

Please wake early from now on. The "typical" person wakes at 7AM on weekdays, but you know what else? The "typical" person ...

- is 15 pounds overweight
- only has 0.8 friends
- has an IQ of only 100
- only earned "B's" and "C's" in high school
- attended college but didn't finish
- only earns $28,000 per year
- is $2,500 in debt ...

Do you want to be average or better than average?

Here's something to be said about above-average people ... what do the CEO's of Disney, Apple, General Motors, Virgin America, and Starbucks share? They're all out of bed by 5:00 AM!

My first reaction to this was, "What a group of workaholics! Glad I'm not one of those ..." Until I discovered that although many successful people wake early to have a "jump" on the day ... the primary reason is for personal, quiet, reflective time.

If you're here, then chances you are:

- A student (you usually wait until the last minute)
- Self-employed (self-motivation is ultra-important)
- Employed (your time is not your own from 8am-5pm)
- A parent (enough said)
- Retired (possibly fixed income, health concerns or time limitations)

Either way, waking even one hour is the solution to most of your problems. In college I discovered firsthand that staying up late or "burning the midnight oil" does NOT work. It only leaves you stressed, tired, overworked, and burned out because you half-ass rush your assignments the night before, or the morning-of, don't you?

On the other hand, here's how I became financially independent (by that I mean property owning and self-employed) ... I woke early, spent about ONE (maybe 1.5) FOCUSED HOURS in the morning, and once that was done, I went in to my day job for 8 hours of loyal servitude. Here's what happened ...

- I separated "church" and "state" – Internet business stays at home, work stays at work
- I actually had time to eat a good breakfast
- I had time for a walk (or a run or swim for the crazy people)

- I began the day with excitement

What's also excellent is after work, I could do other things …
relax, personal time, visit friends and family. This broke me out of
the Work-TV-Sleep cycle most people are stuck in.

I could go on about studies that have shown that the parts of our
brain that affect judgment become tired over the day, which
explains why people overeat, drink, and commit crimes late at
night instead of early in the morning … but let's talk about you!

Sleep Smarter

I'm not saying you have to go to sleep early, or sleep fewer hours,
but you need to be more careful about how you go to sleep …

- Have a set time that you "usually" go to sleep
- Avoid using your computer, TV, phone or iPad one hour
  before sleeping (the glowing light causes sleep problems)
- Your bed is for sleeping only – if you need to nap or
  perform other activities, use your couch
- Sleep in a dark, quiet area that's just a few degrees colder
  than you have during the day (a no brainer but so many
  people miss this)
- Avoid eating right before bed (another no brainer)
- Hypnosis & sleep headphones (my secret weapon)

If I can't sleep or my sleep schedule is out of whack, I use
hypnosis. (I used to experiment with melatonin and valerian root
but it caused more problems than it solved.) Here's what I do …

I put on a pair of sleeping headphones (basically a headband with
thin headphones so you can lay however you want).

I plug the headphone into my iPad, activate airplane mode and open a hypnosis app – I used to use the "BinauralBeat" app but now I use one called "Lucid Dreams."

Hypnosis only works if you let it. It takes about 10-20 minutes for me. The narrator tells me to relax this and that, imagine this and that, breath in this way, count to this number, the next thing I know I wake the next morning and I'm no longer wearing the headphones around my head.

Wake Smarter

Having better sleep habits alone might help you. But we have those days where we don't have time for 8 hours of sleep, or we wake groggy and keep snoozing for 10 more minutes … 10 more minutes … and now you've slept too long and you're running late.

With my limited understanding, we usually wake groggy because our sleep pattern is interrupted. Haven't you slept too long, or had a dream interrupted, and you woke feeling like crap? On the other hand, you've "accidentally" only slept 5 hours and felt fine the next day, because you had your REM sleep and woke during a "light sleep" cycle.

The most amazing iPhone app ever (you can also run if you only own a $99 iPod Touch) is called Sleep Cycle. You place it under your pillow and it "somehow" tracks when you're awake, asleep, or in a deep sleep … based on its gyroscope and the movements you make in bed. You set a 30 minute window for the time you want to wake, and it waits until "the best time" to do it.

- Use "Sleep Cycle" instead of a traditional alarm clock to wake you up

- Get in to the habit of waking at the same time daily
- Get out of bed, out of your bedroom, and preferably outside when you wake
- Use a "Philips GoLite" and several alarm clocks if waking is still a problem
- Don't check e-mail in the morning, relax and be productive instead

Have a Real System

Now that you wake early, you have extra quiet time in the morning to wake, relax, and ready yourself for the day. Once you start your day you'll complete so much even before lunchtime (before anyone has a chance to disrupt you) you'll want to use your time wisely.

I've said this so many times I'm almost sick of it. But this is what you need – FOUR DAILY TASKS.

Have four tasks to complete daily. COMPLETE. Not start, not do, not try, COMPLETE. "Checking e-mail" is not a task. Completing "35% of an e-book" is not a task. Writing one e-book chapter, that's a task. Sending an e-mail to your autoresponder list, that's a money making task. Setting up a web page, that's a task. What works best for me: three 45 minute tasks and one 15 minute task.

Use those three techniques to use your time better, claim your additional 365 days in the year and live longer, and achieve at least double what you did before.

Chapter 16: How to Multiply Yourself

"You don't actually do a project; you can only do action steps related to it. When enough of the right action steps have been taken, some situation will have been created that matches your initial picture of the outcome closely enough that you can call it DONE."
– David Allen

I know that you have been completing your four daily tasks and if you've noticed that you have not necessarily done that today or yesterday or this week, it's time to move back on it. It's time to at once. It's okay to do it at the moment as I'm talking. Write what are the four most important things that you can be doing for the rest of today. Again, as I always recommend that there are three - let's say 45-minute tasks just so we're giving you an actual solid number. If you go over or under that, it's okay. Three 45-minute tasks and one 10-minute task and that's it.

You're not doing 10 things today. You're not doing 20. You're doing whatever the four most important things that will put you in that right direction. Not things necessarily putting out fires or things like checking your Twitter or things necessarily fun but what actually make you the most money and move you in the best most forward direction - for lack of a better term.

Many times, Lance and I will consult someone who has a good long-term plan, someone who maybe wants to make the next yelp.com, the next YouTube, the next Facebook. That's great and we don't want to discourage that by any means, but let's also think about how many sites tried to be Facebook, tried to be MySpace, tried to be YouTube. How many other video sharing sites are there? How many file-sharing sites are there? How many social networks are there that I found even before Facebook?

Think about MySpace, think about LiveJournal, think about Bolt.com, and think about Napster. If some of those sites bring back old memories or if you haven't even heard of those sites, think about why.

For us mere mortals, what we want to do is move towards what is going to make us the most money now so we can receive that money and once the easy stuff is out of the way then we can work on our passion. The best example I could think about is this guy named Bobby Darin who is a musician who had a passion for - I can't remember - but a particular type of music.

What he decided to do was look at what the marketplace wanted, look at what studios wanted and performed a mass-market kind of song. He had some huge hit and he performed the kind of song that would be a hit and make him a lot of money. Once he made that money then he moved onto what he wanted to do. If I'm remembering this right, I think the song "*Beyond the Sea*" from *Finding Nemo*. *Finding Nemo* obviously is a used song but if I remember correctly that was his passion. That style of music, which was a blend of a few different styles had not been done before.

If you're thinking from a real scarcity kind of not a forward-thinking mindset maybe you're thinking, "I only have one of two choices. I could either pursue my passion or I could sell out." But what if you can do both? What if you could do what makes the money now and use that money to then pursue your passion? That way it's a win-win and it gives you a good way of looking at things.

That's something that Lance and I have always done. We don't think of a lot of ideas ourselves as bad that sounds. We look at what our marketplace wants or what we think our best guess is what they want and distribute our product. Sometimes a few things happen. Sometimes we distribute something into the marketplace, something the marketplace needs but does not want or it might be something where the marketplace needs it but maybe the timing is wrong, maybe we've released something two years before it was useful two years after.

An example of that is the tablet. The iPad when it came out it was a huge hit. But everyone forgets that five years before that HP had a tablet, Microsoft had a tablet, all these computer companies, all these laptop makers invented these tablets, but the timing was wrong.

The cause was not there, the technology was not there, the Internet infrastructure was not there. Now, it's cool to have a tablet because you can hold basically the whole computer in your hand and it runs on several gigahertz, holds several gigabytes, runs off Wi-Fi and there's Wi-Fi Internet everywhere, connects the 3G, 4G, all that stuff - the timing is ideal. But an identical product or similar product released a few years before was not a huge hit. Even a few years after the fact, what if everyone has an iPad and some new company comes along and releases a tablet? That's the same as been there, done that as well.

We might put on a product on the marketplace that needs but doesn't want or maybe the timing's wrong or maybe be we just got something wrong with the offer but it's always a guessing game and it's always looking at what the marketplace wants, you do your best, sometimes adjust and sometimes you improve the product or it's time to move on to something else.

What happened with Lance and I was we finished by launching these things called live webinar class. We would say, "I want you to join this course for $1,000. It's going to last four weeks or it's going to last eight weeks. After every week, you'll have this done, this done, this done, and this done. You'll have a product made, a list builder with free subscribers, a sales letter online, and all these various milestones." We taught that that this live class made a good sum.

What we did was turn it around and made those recurring monthly membership sites. That turned out to be a good model for us because if we had it out of the gate decided to make a drip content monthly site, we might not have finished or people might not have actually bought it. But because we could do this thing called a live webinar class, we could test the market, obtain some social proof, adjust the class a quarter of those students, be paid up front, do the next logical step, and create a recurring monthly site.

That worked out as well because we already had a proven system because all these students had used it, we had social proof both inside the members' area and outside. What I mean by that is inside the members' area we had various assignments, various challenges. Sometimes hundreds of people had completed those challenges.

On the outside of the membership site for the sales letter, for the marketing, for the promotion we already had all kinds of proof, case studies, testimonials. Many people who bought the recurring membership site could not afford the high price tag of the live class although they were the same price. What I mean by that is when we run a live class it's usually one payment or maybe split into two or three payments, but it's several hundreds or thousands of dollars.

When we launched a recurring program, it's usually about $100 a month and sometimes even split further down than that. Someone might have looked at that and said, "I can't afford $1,000 once but I can afford $100 monthly and that's something where I can pay as I go." Others might not have had the time or the timing just might not have been right for them to join that class on how to create a video, how to create webinars, how to create a product, how to create membership sites - whatever class we happen to be running - how to create graphics, stuff like that, but now that it was a month or two later now the timing was right.

Today we're going to discuss together how to achieve more, multiply yourself, and double your productivity this week. You look at what we did and you say, "I want to copy that." That's okay. It's okay to look at what we have done and apply that to yourself. But we discussed this before, do you want to make an exact carbon copy, copy and paste clone of Robert and Lance? Do you want to run a live class on membership sites?

Probably not, you're probably going to want to know what skill you have, know what products you have, know what kind of products you could create, know what e-mail subscribers you do have and what they want, what your marketplace wants and now that is the class that you run. So you're not copying, you're just modeling.

What is a model? A model is - for lack of better term - a representation of something complicated into something simple. What you can do is you can say is the model or the business model you guys run using these live webinar classes is figure out what the result will be, chunk it out into four or eight parts, step those out in the modules, figure out what the price is going to be, you receive a stack of traffic to a live webinar, pitch that webinar, keep pitching it, keep following it up with your best customers, fill that class so it's a sum you are happy with like $10,000, $20,000, $30,000, put in one or two hours a week showing up on the live class and present that one lesson for about an hour.

At the end have an assignment, do the assignment with them, follow up two times, and once you're done it doesn't have to be any more complicated than that. Now they have what you promised. If you can make it fit together and have a logical systematic sequence then that is excellent as well. Now you can turn around and set up an affiliate program, run it monthly. Even with that there are even more things you can do.

For example, when we run a live webinar class we're busy with the teaching part. But once that class is over sometimes we'll think about software I can add or I will restructure the membership area so it makes a lot more sense. I will make a physical version of that product. I will transcribe the videos and make a printed set of manuals.

Let's say that someone joins our six-month course and they dropped out after month three, then we'll do this thing called the reactivation campaign where those who have gone halfway through our membership site and dropped out, we'll give them a special button to rejoin and complete their remaining payments, because many times people don't notice the bill or decided they can't afford it at the moment or their credit card expires. Plenty of reasons for people to drop out of your membership site so why not give them the opportunity or at least the idea to returning.

There's this thing called modeling. It's like copying, only you're looking at what didn't work and what did work and I'm going to not copy what did not work and I will copy what did work. This relates to everything, not just with the business but also with yourself and with things like being happy, being productive and making money, moving in the right direction, all of that stuff. That's called being in the right state, being in a productive state.

Most people when they're in a productive state, it's all similar across the board. They are not frowning, they're probably smiling. They're alert, they're sitting up straight. For many people they're standing as I do sometimes. For many people they are typing with the computer. That is a productive state.

Instead of having to think about here is how I'm smiling, here's how I'm sitting, here's how I'm breathing - too many variables. Let's instead simplify it and think about a state. I'm going to take out a piece of paper here and let's think about what state do you want to be in? I'm talking about what are the emotions? Should I be angry, scared, blah, blah. What state do you want to be in? Maybe you want to be in a productive state, maybe you want to be in a certainty state - that's another mode you can be in - and maybe creativity state.

At some point, you want to be productive and just finish it. Other times you just want to be in a certainty state where you want confidence like running a webinar, for example. Other times creativity state like coming across certain roadblocks, figuring out why launch shouldn't go so well, figuring out your product. The more I think about it, those three states are all we need immediately, maybe even ever.

You think about productivity, certainty, and creativity. With productivity, we can look at this from a few angles. First, what memories do you have of being productive? Another thing about that is what conditions were you in? What location were you in? Were you in your office? Was it a particular time of day? Were your certain distractions removed? Did you have water or energy drink? We have your memory, you have conditions.

Let's even go into your imagination. I'm going to draw another branch coming out of that bubble. We're thinking about what's the visual component? What's the audio component? What's the kinesthetic component out of that? By visual, think back to when you were in a productive state. If that state could be a color what would it be? If that state could be a shape or if it could be a movie or if it could be a picture or if it could be several pictures, what would that productive state look like?

I've told you in the past that for me a productive state is where there's a blue, pleasant haze. It's like a warm area and there is a security cam footage of me typing away on a desk. It's a giant me in a tiny desk and there's one giant image of that with a thick white border and a bit of a drop shadow. At the moment at least, there are a few smaller Polaroid similar to that kind of almost orbiting but it's moving slowly. It's moving towards the right, towards the up direction. I was talking about what kind of motion is going on in that picture, in that movie and that's a good place to start. What does that productive state look like?

Next is audio, what does that productive state sound like? An easy thing of that is, is there music or is there quietness? Is there a hum? Is there a background noise? Are there sound effects or is there a speech? Is there anything going on in the background? For me, if I think about what does a productive state sound like? If I think back to that, I think about in my imagination or memory what did that sound like, I think about not necessarily my heart beating but my brain going whoo-whoo. It's like my whole body is alive and pulsing.

Then we think about the kinesthetic part. What did that productive state feel like? Let's think about the temperature - the coolness, the warmth. Let's think about body parts. Let's think about what parts of you - no dirty jokes now please - but what parts of you feel more alive or feel like something's happening. At least what I'm thinking about my productive state, my core is rotating or in a state of good unrest, if that make sense. That's your state.

You could look at all these variables. All these things together equals a productive state. All I have to do to put myself in a productive state is think back to what it did look like, sound like, feel like. What was I doing? What are my thoughts and what was my body positioned like? I guess part of the kinesthetic is what is your body physiology, your positioning, your posture, all that good kind of stuff. We do the same thing for things like certainty, things like creativity.

I'm not saying that you have to always to be crazy. You might notice at the moment I'm alert, I'm intense, but am I crazy flying off the handle? Not really. I'm tired. I'm not at my 100% best, but I am alert, I'm focused, I'm in the moment, and I'm excited. But I'm not saying, "I'm excited! I'm not exploding immediately." I'm toned down excited, which is still okay. That's your productive state.

Now we think about a state of certainty. For me, an easy one for that always happens daily? I think about things like the sun coming up. That's always going to happen daily. You sitting out of bed - that's something that always happens daily. For me, thinking about breathing, a calm breathing. I guess you could always have a state of calm, but at the moment we're talking about productivity so screw the state of calm. Being calm comes naturally. Same thing with certainty.

If you can think back to a time when you saw the sun coming up, think about a time when you looked at your watch. Think about a time when you sat at your computer and everything was ideal, in order, and excellent. What did that look like, sound like, feel like? What was going on literally in the moment and what were the conditions in and around you?

With creativity, let's think about what like a frowned moment. Now we're going in the opposite. What's something that doesn't happen daily? What's an epiphany you had or a breakthrough you had at some point? What did that feel like?

Let's think about the first time you thought of the name for your first product. Heck, if you want to be personal, when you thought of a name for your first child. What about the time when you decided to quit that one job or you decided to take that huge risk and it paid off? Again, what was the moment? What did it feel like, sound like, look like? What do you remember and what were your surroundings like? These are all states.

It's always one of those things where you have various techniques and what you do at first is you want to think always work, always work. But your brain becomes used to it and we outsmart our subconscious, as funny as that sounds. You have these things called states and to easily and more frequently return to those states, all these stimuli, this is all anchoring. You think back to a productive time and place, your imagination is based on reality. So when you were productive, you did see these things, you did hear these things somehow and they became linked, so now by seeing and hearing these things in your imagination you relinked it. These are things called anchoring.

The easy anchor is smiling. You're used to when you're happy, you smile. So when you want to be happy again, you smile, then you become happy. When you sit at your desk, if your desk is always clean, you always feel focused and not overwhelmed and excited to conquer the day then every time you sit at your desk then things will feel simple, you'll feel excited, you do the next thing.

The reason that many relationships fail, many breakups happen is that you go through the same fight repeatedly with someone or you go through the same kind of argument or the same kind of anguish repeatedly with someone and you reach where you associate seeing that person with being in that crappy state, crappy mood. That's why that person makes you unhappy. You don't know why, but time to break up. The opposite is true if you go with someone and you have similar experiences. You go to various places, have a good time, then it goes the other way, it goes in the positive way.

Anchoring is, again, really powerful, really easy to go either way. This is an easy way to tap into that productive state. It's wonderful to start but you become used to it and here's what I mean. People will start to realize this thing anchoring is really easy. It's pop myself into this other state. If I want to be happy, let me keep saying I'm happy. Let me write it down a hundred times that I'm happy, then I'll believe it or let me write a hundred times, read it, speak it out and repeat it aloud a hundred times.

That will work for a while until you go the other way. You end by dissociating from it if you said you were happy a hundred times every hour. Your brain will become used to you doing this and your body would start realizing that whether I'm happy, I keep saying I'm happy. As it's less and less effective over time, then you start to realize that now it makes no difference. I'm being an idiot. I'm saying I'm happy a hundred times. I'm writing I'm happy a hundred times whether I'm happy. At the end of that, I'm still not happy or maybe I am but it doesn't make a change so now it's dissociated. These are these things called affirmations, which always sound good.

Don't you know someone who knows everything about a particular subject but they're terrible? I don't want to insult any teachers, but don't you know a smart mathematics teacher who can only find a job as a mathematics teacher. Don't you know a good relationship expert who's single? Of course, they're all over the place proof that it's possible to know all the facts, know all the rules, know all the right stuff but still not apply it.

Am I saying I'm an expert? Of course not, I'm just a computer programmer. I used to have problems of my own but I've overcome a lot of stuff by using these tools. Don't discount these because they're still useful tools. But if you noticed that one tool is not doing the job then you have to switch to different tools.

That's why we talk about many various things because one strategy in particular is not going to solve your problems. Maybe it will for a while, but life is always changing, we always have to figure out what's next. Why am I at where I'm at? Why am I headed in that direction? How can I change the direction that I'm in?

That's useful I think in looking at not just where you're at now but did you come from, where are you going and thinking more steps ahead, being more a self-aware person and basically - for lack of a better term, I hope this isn't a phrase - but playing chess instead of playing checkers. Let's think about what that means.

Again, I hate to insult any group of people in particular. Some of our customers – a small percentage - some of them are rude. I'm thinking about one guy in particular and Lance, if he's listening, will probably know whom I'm talking about. We deal with this guy weekly. He happens to change his name weekly and relocate to a different continent every week, in a different country to obtain a different credit card. Basically, there's usually one rude person a week but it's always the same personality type.

This person comes in and maybe he has one problem with us, maybe he bought and the download link didn't quite work or he installed a plugin, it didn't quite install quite right or he couldn't figure out how to use one feature or he bought assuming a particular feature that wasn't actually there or not understanding what the software did - for whatever reason, he is slightly unhappy. He comes in guns blazing, rude, and shouting, demands, threats "I'm going to refund, help me now," we don't respond within an hour, "help me now" again.

We're professional about it, we're patient about it, we're not passive or anything like that. We do solve the problem, but a day later, he is yelling at us about this or about that - nothing will please this person.

Maybe you've dealt with that kind of person in your life. Actually, I guarantee you have where nothing you say will help. Some of these people they'll yell at you, say their piece, they'll be done, and they run out of steam. But others, that'll just keep them going and there's nothing you can do. The important thing to remember is that it's not your fault, it's not about you, it's them.

I don't 100% understand it but what I think is going on is there's this thing called cognitive dissonance. That means if you say that you're hungry, if you say that you're grumpy then your mind and your body is going to do its best to stay in line with that. As a person, you don't like contradicting yourself. No one likes to be a hypocrite.

First, they shout and we help them regardless if they shout or not. By the way, if you're one of our customers, please don't shout. We'll still help you. I'm not going to hold it against you. They shout and we help them. The first thing that happens is they anchor, they link or it's already been linked that shouting and being rude helps them with what they perceived to be faster, better service, the first misconception.

The other thing that happens is they come in angry and shouting. It's easier to stay where you're at. They come in unhappy and the problem is fixed but they're still committed to being this unhappy person. Although the problem's been fixed and there's no reason to be rude and unhappy, they're still in this rude or unhappy state. They're still that rude and unhappy person. Their whole day is like this I think.

It's easy to become stuck so they devise new reasons to stay grumpy, stay unhappy, and stay unsatisfied. We fix everything with their problem, now the service was too slow or now the problem is that the font size is wrong, it doesn't look quite right.

This probably will sound slightly bitchy and I hope that's not so. but what we see many people doing is they become stuck in basically these primal habits and they move in this mind state of "I'm unhappy so I'm going to do whatever I possibly can to stay that way", which is a silly thing. I'm not s, sometimes I'll be in an unhappy feedback loop and I'll say, "Why am I in this loop? What started it?" If what started it is gone then there's no reason to be unhappy.

How do you then leave that state? You can't just snap out of it. That doesn't work. You have to be cleverer than that. I think - a couple of things. First, changing your state, taking a breath, stopping what you're doing, walking out of the house, clearing your head, putting the phone away, taking a walk - all those things first reset your brain and make you rethinking things.

The other thing is usually there's an underlying cause. It's one of those things where if you're home life is unhappy, then your work suffers and vice versa. If there's that one thing you've been putting off and it's been nagging you, our brains are complicated. Often some things bother you and you don't even realize that they are bothering you.

An ideal example for me is when I'm about to leave on a trip like the day or day or two before, I'll be leaving on a trip I'm just constantly in a panicky kind of feeling. It makes no sense because I'm thinking I'm not worried about the plane crashing, I'm not worried about anything going wrong while I'm away, I'm not worried about anything that happening while I'm there. There's no reason for me to be stressed out, it's just that that's how I am at that point. When I'm about to travel, going on a new trip, I am stressed out.

I have to manage my state better and use one of these tools such as a pattern interrupt or clearing my head to deal with that, to not ignore it, to not counter it or circulate it but ride it out and have an easy time enough during that day. Then I'll go on my trip and when I leave, I'll be fine.

People live their lives based on that necessity or based on those possibilities – people who live their lives based on "What am I reacting to?" versus "What I am proactively doing?" Reacting means that every time I'm about to leave on a trip I become stressed, I lash out, everyone hates me, makes me hate myself, involve myself in all these fights, what I did in younger days.

But now I'm more aware this is going to be a problem. I tell everyone I'm about to travel, I'm going to be stressed but not too much because we don't want to say, "I'm going to be super-stressed," because guess what, you said it, now you'll be super-stressed. I'll be 10% more stressed than normal but I'm going to muddle through, I'm going to do this, this, this and this to counteract it. I'll be more aware of it. I'll make it more a point to do this anchoring, to do the smiling. I'll keep myself more occupied with work. I will pack before time to make sure that I'm ready to go and have a few stressful things as possible. We're thinking ahead, and we're being smarter about it.

Speaking of that, speaking of thinking ahead, and being smarter - procrastination. We've also discussed this. Let's say you're procrastinating about one thing. I know most of you procrastinate about several things but let's think about that one thing that you're procrastinating the most on. You know what it is because you just thought of it, didn't you? By the most I mean not necessarily the biggest problem or the most recent problem, but what's the most important thing for you to fix at once. It might be something you can fix this week or today, then that'll just be one fewer pebble in your shoe basically.

Procrastination means something that you have to do but you can't bring yourself to do it. The reason is that you have to. It's something that it is required but it's not that fun, not that pleasant and you don't see much of a reward and upside to it. Of course, you're not going to do it because you make all these judgments. In a courtroom or whatever where there's like the statue with the blindfold and the two weights, judging means you weigh two things. Whichever one is lighter, is easier, that's what you go with.

Procrastination means that you should go to the dentist because if you don't then you'll have cavities, you'll have yellow teeth, and your teeth will shift. Those are the reasons to go. The reasons not to go, because the dentist costs money, takes time out of your day, it's scary, it's painful, you might be ashamed because what if they find a cavity or they say you didn't clean enough? Way more reasons not to go. You have to turn "haves" into "should" into "wants" to choose to go to the dentist, to want to go to the dentist and you go from having to go to the dentist as if it's a necessity to knowing you should go to the dentist into now you want to go to the dentist.

Why would anyone want to do the dishes? Why would anyone want to go to the dentist? Let's think about this. You're turning your "have" into a "should." We said we have to go to the dentist because if you don't you'll have cavities. Why should you go to the dentist? Because it's the right thing to do, because it's a good habit to start and if you start going at present and return to that pattern of going every six months then that will be good for you. You should go to the dentist because you'll live longer and because, yes, it will cost you money but in the long run it'll cost you less money because you don't need dentures or root canal or any kind of other painful surgery. You just go regularly and they will clean it up.

If you have a family then you're setting a good example and hey, it's not all about you, is it? You take them along, you have their teeth cleaned as well - sure, maybe they will hate you then but maybe you can take satisfaction in knowing that you're all in it together and that everyone is benefiting.

You should go to the dentist for all those reasons but you're still not quite there. You need to turn a should into a want, so why would you want to go to the dentist? You want to go to the dentist because you want to have it out of the way. You want it to stop nagging at you and you know what, you know that once you go to that dentist that you will feel better about yourself and you will know that you achieved something that wasn't easy to do, that the typical person would avoid doing, but you went ahead, and did it. Is it that bad? Is it going to make fun of you?

Maybe, maybe not. But if they do, that just might be their personality that might be their way of making you do better. If it's bad, then next time, don't go to that dentist. One thing that helps me so much in life is that you'll never have to see this person again. Think about that.

If you're dealing with a rude bartender, a rude person at a hotel, a rude person at Starbucks, you'll never have to see that person ever again for the rest of your existence - ever. It's interesting. Turn your haves and shoulds into wants, then those will develop into long-term recurring habits of always going to the dentist and being okay with it.

Traveling and not being stressed out, launching products consistently so it feels weird if this week you didn't launch your product, posting to your blog once a month so it feels weird if you didn't post monthly, and overall, just completing things. I think it's important for you to complete things that you start and realize that if there's something that you didn't complete or didn't start then it wasn't that important to begin with.

I know that I'm giving you a lot of this advice and some of you were taking it and agreeing with everything and some of you are poking holes in everything I say and trying to find an excuse for why that doesn't apply to you. We've also discussed this kind of person. We have matchers who see similarities in the world and we have mismatchers who see differences in the world and that's another way of being smarter than yourself and knowing who you are.

That way, if you find yourself always disagreeing with yourself or being kind of having that inner conflict, it's because you keep finding differences in everything, okay but let's use that to our advantage, which means again that if you need a good reason to launch your product, maybe it's because you want to be different and better than everyone else. Not every product is the same. Although there may be products on affiliate marketing, you can have your own spin on it. Not every launch is the same and it's going to be interesting to see how this adventure you're about to embark on is going to play out.

You have matchers and mismatchers and you're motivated by pleasure and by pain. That dentist example was ideal. At first I listed all these ways of basically pain-based motivation. We said things like, "It won't be that bad." We said things like, "The dentist might insult you, make fun of you. It might hurt, it might cost money." But we then focus on the pleasure. It will cost less money in the long run and it even hit you, "So what?" and all that. You're motivated by pleasure and by pain and I think it's important to shake things up many times.

If you notice that you're stuck in a loop, stuck in a rut, stuck in the same habits, it's because your pleasure and your pain have been balanced or have been listed or had the same score board this whole time. What I mean by that is quitting my day job. I had reasons to quit, reasons not to quit. Reasons to quit was because I needed it, was because I needed that growth, needed more money, needed more free time, I wanted to go on more adventures.

Reasons not to quit, off the top my head, were things like stability, health insurance, and social interaction. Those factors hadn't changed but you just change one factor, then the whole scale is moved. Think about that.

If you have two weights on the scale and they're similar, you change this one side by five or ten pounds and zoom, suddenly everything tips in the other direction. What did I do to quit my day job? I got health insurance and the reason I got health insurance is that I wanted to go to a seminar and my schedule simply wouldn't allow it. Hmm, interesting that the pleasure drives us more.

Pain and pleasure - they are more powerful than the other in their different ways but I've noticed that pain is always there and pain drives us in a particular way but we end resenting the pain, if that make sense. I think a better place to be is to be motivated by what could happen, to be motivated by something I want to go out and do to grow, to move to the next chapter in my life, and I'm going to have to finally go across this tiny hurdle to reap these huge rewards.

We're talking about modeling, we're talking about improving your life and I want to mention to you the best, the first, and the most successful self-help book ever published called "How to Win Friends and Influence People." It's a dull read because it's out of date and I think many people have said what's in this book, they said it's better since then.

Listening to this book, I use a service called Audible where you pay $15 a month. You receive a free book to listen to monthly so it's cheaper than paying $50 every time you want an audio book. You can download it so you don't have to throw anything away or keep it on the bookshelf.

I was listening to this book and it's old but the recurring pattern I got at this entire book was don't think so much about yourself. Think more about how the other person would see things and by thinking a few steps behind, a few steps ahead, if that make sense, then you go a long way as far as not necessarily being right but achieving what you want out of people. Again, not manipulatively but you'll move along better and everybody wins. You'll achieve what you want, they'll achieve what they want. In the past, it was a situation of neither of you achieves what you want because you're both selfish and pig-headed.

Let me list through the various lessons because it's all you need. He tells story after story and the story ended with a lesson so it becomes ingrained in you. You don't have to memorize the bullet point, you remember the whole story. But let me condense this into a few points here.

In reality, there are four techniques for handling people, six ways to then make them like you and 12 ways to win people to your way of thinking. You might have heard this also explained as know, like, and trust.

How to "Know"

1) Don't criticize, condemn or complain.

2) Give honest and sincere appreciation.

3) Arouse in the other person an eager wants.

4) Never show disinterest.

Pain vs. pleasure motivator: If someone was stealing your car would you put more effort into saving that soul in the car or into buying a new car? You'd be on the survival mode, the scarcity mode, you'd be more inclined to avoid pain. It's tempting and many of us focus and put in managerial terms. It's tempting to motivate others working for you, working with you to motivate them based on threats, to motivate them based on pain.

That might work at first but that only takes you so far and it ends by working where you attract more flies with honey than with vinegar. If you reward someone for a job well done then they'll have a good feeling. That will be a drug and they'll want to repeat that instead of being the drill sergeant where it works for a while. But with drill sergeant, boot camp is only what six weeks, eight weeks - it doesn't last forever and once you are past that point then you're more rewarded as far as I understand it for good things. That's the know part. Don't threat, don't be a jerk, reward for good things.

How to "Like"

1) Become genuinely interested in others.

2) Smile and that's because if you smile, they smile, it makes everyone's day better.

3) Remember that a person's name is to that person the sweetest and most important sound in any language.

4) Be a good listener, encourage others to talk about themselves.

5) Talk about the other person's interest.

6) Make the other person feel important and do it sincerely.

It's kind of interesting that this section builds on the previous section where in the previous section we said don't criticize, condemn or complain, give honest and sincere appreciation, arouse in the other person and eager wants, never show others that you are not interested in what they have to say. It ended with now we're going to listen to that person, but this one turned into become genuinely interested in others, smile, use their name, be a good listener, and talk in their other interest. That means learn what they like to know and that way you can talk about their home turf, talk about their subjects that they like to talk about, then make the other person feel important.

This whole section is not always about you. What you want is there but you'll achieve more of what you want if you can give them what they want, if that makes sense. You'll achieve a lot more everywhere with the friendship, with the marriage, with business if you have attitude of giving and not just taking.

If you have a book, you have a course you want to teach, you want to help as many people as possible, use the information and not necessarily sell many copies of your book. If it's that kind of situation where I have a sales letter or I have a pitch then yes, I want to sell copies of my books but I'm not being too stingy about what I do and don't reveal.

If someone pays for a course of mine, then that benefits everyone involved compared with giving it away free because if I am paid for my effort, for my training, for my materials then I can make more and I can have the time to support my materials. Because someone's bought a product from me they have skin in the game, now they have a good reason to make their investment pay and they'll give a value to it instead of receiving something free.

That's why I call that the know section. I'm sorry, that was the like section. The first section was the know section. You get people to know you or you get to know them by motivating them in the right way, listening to them. Now we're at the like section where you're relating directly to them, you're aligning yourself with their beliefs and their interests.

How to "Trust"

Again, if we compare this to Attention-Interest-Desire-Action, it's the same thing. The first section was interest or attention. Now we're in interest, let's move to desire or what we should call the trust area, 12 ways to win people to your way of thinking.

1) The only way to win the best of an argument is to avoid it. To me, that means would you rather be right or be happy?

2) Show respect for the other person's opinions. Never bluntly say, "You're wrong."

3) If you are wrong, admit it quickly and emphatically. This relates a lot to a guy named Joe Sugarman where if you say the wrong thing or you make a mistake or if you have a product where it has an obvious flaw, then admit it so it doesn't make a big deal.

4) Begin in a friendly way.

5) Start with questions to which the other person will answer yes.

Later in history, Robert Cialdini would call this commitment and consistency. Keep asking questions where someone will keep saying, "Yes, this makes sense. Yes, this makes sense. Yes, this makes sense." Boom, got the sale.

If I say, "I'm selling a course on webinars," I'm saying, "Do you want to make the most sales of your product?" "Yes."

"Do you want the most involved buyers or potential buyers of your product altogether in one place?" "Yes."

"Do you want to sell high ticket and be able to have everything in a compressed scarcity launch?" "Yes."

"Do you see most other product creators running their own webinars?" "Yes."

"Don't you want to be like this product creator?" "Yes."

"Then doesn't it make sense for you to run a webinar?" "Yes."

If I said off the bat, "Should you run a webinar?" the answer is "I don't know" or it's "No" but because I did all these baby steps and said yes the entire way, now it makes sense.

6) Let the other person do most of the talking. This ties neatly back into talking about which product should I make, what should I teach in the class, what should the sales letter be, the majority of that is revising, is I put an offer on the table and depending on what people want - I don't just base on the person but what I'm seeing the entire marketplace or my entire subscriber base wants - I will adjust the offer accordingly.

7) Let the other person feel the idea is his or hers. This is the movie Inception.

8) Try honestly to see things from the other person's point of view.

9) Be sympathetic with the other person's ideas and desires.

10) Appeal to the nobler motives.

11) Dramatize your ideas.

12) Throw down a challenge.

We said, the only way to win the best out of an argument is to avoid it - number one. Number two, show respect for other people's opinion, never say you're wrong. Number three, if you are wrong admit it quickly and emphatically. Number four, begin in a friendly way. Number five, start with a question to which the other person will answer yes. Number six, let the other person do most of the talking. Number seven, let the other person feel the idea is his or hers. Number eight, try honestly to see things from the other person's point of view. Number nine, be sympathetic with the other person's ideas and desires. Number 10, appeal to the nobler motives. Number 11, dramatize your ideas. And number 12, throw down a challenge.

There's even more. There's ones about being a leader, which are derivatives of these but that's a lot of stuff to remember. Those are 22 different points, so much stuff. It's okay because this was the first self-help book in history.

How do we make sense of all these? This guy named Joe Sugarman, a smart guy, I met him once, came out with a book called "Triggers", which outlines 30 different motivators to entice people to buy – such as greed, authority, justifying something with logic, exclusivity like a private club, scarcity, many various things and it's the same as a similar format where he tells story after story.

He'll tell one story where I think one of the earliest ones is he's at an ice-cream shop and he wants a hot fudge sundae. It's at a particular price and it's too high a price for his liking.

He says, "Hey, can I have ice cream?" It's half that price.

The waitress says, "Sure."

He says, "By the way, can I have some fudge on top?"

She says, "Yes."

He got a hot fudge sundae for half price because he snuck that extra thing in. That's a lesson on commitment and consistency.

He did other things such as - he was flying on a flight from Hawaii, Honolulu to San Francisco across the Pacific Ocean and there was a problem with the plane. The pilots, the airline they were secretive. They didn't want to tell the passengers what the problem was, what the delay was.

But because this guy, Joe Sugarman, is a pilot of his own he overheard what the problem was and he asked if he could address the passengers. He said the problem is with the plane, it's this thing and the problem is just that. There's an electric problem and they can't refuel the plane while engines are running and don't worry the pilots are even more afraid than you and I and it's not a plane-threatening problem.

Suddenly, everyone was about to cancel their flights and they said, "Okay, now were going to fly the plane," and everything worked out. The airline covered up the problem, it hurt them and if they had just explained in simple terms what the problem was and said, "There is a problem," it doesn't matter.

I think the underlying thread, the pattern throughout the book called "*Triggers*" is that if there's a problem with your offer or your service or with everything, explain it in a way that it does not matter. Yes, it exists, we're not going to ignore it. We're not going to try to circulate it or convict someone they're wrong, but let's ignore it. Again, "*Triggers*," there are 30 different things. It's a lot to take in.

This other guy named Robert Cialdini, a smart guy because his first name is Robert (just kidding), if I remembered right, he went undercover as a used car salesman. Let's simplify this even more. Let's figure what motivates people to act and buy and agree with you and do what you want, what influences them, what makes them motivated and become productive. He reduced this to six things. I don't know about you, but you know going from 22 and 30, six things is a lot easier for me.

Let's list out what are these called "Cialdini Weapons of Influence." Those things are authority, liking, reciprocity, commitment and consistency, scarcity, and always leave off one, social proof. What do these mean? We'll go through them real quick.

Authority means that someone respects you. They respect you, they trust you enough to listen to what you have to say.

Liking - you're similar enough that what you have to say is actually relevant. They can relate to you somehow. A good example of this is Mitt Romney or some of these rich guys like Bill Gates or someone like that. Can you relate to Donald Trump, Mitt Romney, and Bill Gates? Not really because they have a lot more money than you in their everyday life. Richard Branson's everyday life is not like yours. Then again, your local politician or your best friend or someone you know from work, if they're on the same economic class as you like someone you know in business, your business partner, they're on a similar income level as you, if they're on the same geographic area, similar age, similar situation, then now there's more liking to that person because you can relate.

Reciprocity - simple, I give to you and you give back to me. I'm going to write the word "give" next to that.

Commitment and consistency - that's the whole thing where I'm going to say keep saying yes. As we said, you keep asking yes questions.

You say, "Do you see you running webinars?"

"Yes."

"If all there was to running a webinar was starting the computer, hitting a button, showing the screen of a PowerPoint, and talking - if that's all you have to do, do you think you could do that?"

"Yes."

"Okay, now you can run this because everyone else does it, it's effective and it's easy for you to use as well."

On a stage presentation then we might do something where I'll have someone keep raising their hand every few minutes not to manipulate but just to make it easier to understand. If they keep agreeing to what I'm saying then they more actively listen and yes, at the end they'll actually buy.

Scarcity: I'm going to put limit number of copies. Sometimes we need to give someone a real reason to act, buy immediately and do something immediately. That might mean that if we're running a live webinar class, it will only be this price until tomorrow. We're only going to allow 10 students and that's it and if they missed out, if they don't buy, then it's closed up well, next launch you had better believe that they will buy.

Social proof - real simple. Testimonials. I'm going to write that but it's also social proof, reviews, seeing others do it.

Those are the six things that entice people to buy. I think that out of all the lessons I read for you from "How to Win Friends and Influence People," from the Joe Sugarman's "Triggers," those can all be reduced to those six things.

One other way of making sense of this, because what I then tacked onto this was this guy Tony Robbins who has this thing called "Six Human Needs" and in our Video Sales Tactics course we tied it together. Tony Robbins' six human needs are certainty, variety, love, significance, growth, and contribution.

First, those six Cialdini weapons, those are ways of making people do what we want, but these six human needs these are what we do want. Certainty means security, stability, variety that's like adventure. Love is like connection with others. Significance is recognition and credit for what we do. Growth is things improving over time. Contribution is the greater good, it's also improving over time.

I've tried figuring out ways of fitting these together, maybe I should have a grid and figure out where authority intersects with significance or with social proof, it interacts with certainty, and it doesn't fit together that well. I'm mentioning this to you for a few different reasons.

It's because what we're talking about today is how to achieve more, multiply yourself and double your productivity this week and you'll double your productivity by having more focused batch and enjoyable work time. You'll have a better life in general if instead of reacting to every little roadblock or instead of becoming caught in those loops that interrupt your pattern and quit those nasty bad habits. You'll be able to do that by knowing, first, based on your six human needs what's the most important in your life.

For many, if you're later in life, certainty is probably more important than variety. Your cash flow will keep going in or that the assets you own you'll keep hanging onto. If you have a family versus not having a family, love is more important. If you're more a career business oriented person then significance and growth might be more important.

You have to know yourself and you have to know what your priorities are and what the most important thing is. That way, if you have to choose between having a day job versus building a business for yourself, if you value variety and your freedom and growth more than certainty and love, then stay in your day job.

One thing that I will tell you is that when I went full time I lost some friends, as when I graduated from college I lost some friends. It's as when I started college I lost friends, as when I graduated in high school I lost friends, it's as when I started high school I lost friends. Because every time you change your surroundings and your friends also change, it has that ripple effect.

When you're aligning your pain versus your pleasure, you're figuring out, "I'm trying to turn my haves into shoulds into wants," I'm saying what are the reasons to do something, the reasons not to do something, now you can use these various weapons of influence as justification. Here's what I mean. You can use authority on yourself because you know all these facts about what will happen if you do or you don't go to the dentist. You can use liking because you can say, "Which of my friends go to the dentist?" All of them, so that means I should as well.

Reciprocity: If I go to the dentist then I will reward myself by buying that new video game or going out to the movies or buying that new e-book. You reward yourself, you're reciprocating, you're giving something and receiving something in return.

Commitment and Consistency: If you have been going to the dentist regularly, you got that habit, then it's easy to keep that habit going and yes, it might be difficult to a new habit started but once it started then it's something that you'll continuously be doing.

Scarcity is present because if you wait then you'll have a cavity. It is important you do it now. For me, most sales scarcity comes into play because I know that in a week or even in an hour, chances are I won't be as motivated or inclined or even thinking about if I should go. I've already talked myself out of it.

Do it now before you think of a reason to talk yourself out of it.

Social Proof: after you go to the dentist, who can you brag to or how can you feel better? After you go to the dentist, how will your social and your life improve and change? You have fresher breath, you have whiter teeth - all that good stuff.

I've told you repeatedly that all these persuasion techniques they apply much in online sales, but they also apply just as well I think in motivating yourself and making yourself do those things that you know are going to happen. It's not a matter even of things that you choose to have happened but it's your destiny.

You're going to end at point B, you're at point A at the moment. You know what your goals are going to be. You know that you want to distribute this information product. You know that it's going to make you X amount of money and it might take you all to figure it out, but you know you'll make a particular sum and it will be enough to pay your chilrens' college education. It will be enough to move to a better house, repay your house, go on vacation or whatever it is, you know it's going to happen.

It's a certainty. You're an unstoppable machine. I believe in you and it's just a matter of figuring out that middle part. That's always the tricky part. You know where you are at the moment, you know where you want to be, then you have to backtrack to figure out "Now I have to fill those few years of those decades to reach where my goals are." It doesn't sound too out there.

Know where you want to be – that's the most important thing. Model others who have taken that path with you. Move in the right state, so that's one fewer thing to worry about. Anchor yourself to always reach where you want to go. Use these tools. Affirmation is not too much. Be more inclined about what could happen instead of what has happened or what is happening. Be proactive and avoid that temptation of reacting. Acquire good habits. Weigh the pleasure and the pain. Interrupt your pattern.

Use these tools like Cialdini - authority, liking, reciprocity, commitment and consistency, scarcity, and social proof - to make others do what you want and more important, to allow you to do what you want. Remember the six human needs so you know what's important to you and where you are and where you're headed - certainty, variety, love, significance, growth, and contribution.

I want you to list four things that we haven't already, four things that you are going to do for certain today - not tomorrow. Don't plan your whole week, your whole month. What are the four most important things in your business, not in your life? What are four things?

We're saying three 45-minute tasks and one 10-minute task. You can list down at present in incomplete sentence, not even a full sentence, share with someone else so that will make sure you do it, then report when you're done.

What did that do? You shared it with someone else, so that gives you your social proof if you did or you didn't do it.

Scarcity. You have to do it today because it's today's task. If you don't do them today then either important things aren't completed or they weren't important in the first place.

Commitment and Consistency. I'm telling you to do four simple tasks to complete today and tomorrow you'll have four tasks completed as well.

Reciprocity. You do these four tasks and you know what that will give you? Four things that were done that you probably wouldn't have completed before.

Liking. This is like all those times when you know you needed to have something done and you had that good day where it felt like an easy day but you got those most important things done. This has also worked for many of my other students and I know it's going to work for you because it works for me as well.

Authority. I'm telling you immediately, when you took the time to examine this entire chapter, I know that you know, like, and trust and at least respect me that we're friends, that we're working together, you're on my team. This is my number-one secret. This is my number-one tool. This is what has always worked for me and always will work, it works for everyone I know who tried it, the only catch is when they stop doing it, and it stops working. Imagine that.

Go out there and make me proud. Do your four daily tasks. Tell someone you're going to do it. Go ahead, and do them. Go back and report to that person for whom you completed those four things.

Chapter 17: How to Pull Confidence Out of Thin Air

"It is surely a great calamity for a human being to have no obsessions."
– Bob Bly

I was talking to someone the other night who dreaded to run a webinar. Many people are. Many of you have "enough" technical skills to do it, enough knowledge of your topic to present, but "something" is holding you back.

Let's change that for you, immediately!

Again, I am NOT a self-help expert of any kind. But I have run 359 live webinars (697 hours) so I know a few things about webinar confidence and public speaking.

You and I both have our own unique set of problems. Let's solve those problems for you, not in one huge step but in a few SMALL pieces at a time …

News Flash: You Have Only Have 8 Emotions (Seriously!)

As a nerdy computer programmer, I like to take apart what makes us work. And according to psychologists (I'm not one and haven't read ANY books about psychology) you have 8 basic emotions:

- joy
- trust
- anticipation
- surprise

- fear
- anger
- sadness
- disgust

That's it! Anything else you feel is either one of these in greater or lesser intensity (namely, rage, jealousy, distraction, annoyance, interest) or is a combination of these (namely, love or guilt).

"But dammit Jim, I'm a computer programmer, not a psychologist." That "psychology" explanation looks like a group of ideas thrown at me. I like to deconstruct and simplify things.

This information isn't available in any book, only right here. At least not assembled in the way I've done it here. Let's put it into a systematic formula you can apply today.

Eight things are a lot to keep track of … are four key concepts easier? Of course, they are. So let's remember that each of these 8 emotions has an OPPOSITE … for example, the opposite of being "happy" is "sad", right?

Four Positives and Four Negatives

That means you really only have four negative and four positive states:

ANTICIPATION (positive) <–> SURPRISE (positive)

JOY (positive) <–> sadness (negative)

TRUST (positive) <–> disgust (negative)

FEAR (negative) <–> anger (negative)

(I've put positive emotions in ALL CAPS and negative ones in lower caps to make this more readable.)

The "green" and "orange" colors don't mean good or bad, it's just so you can tell which the opposites of one another are. For example, "joy" and "sadness" are opposites because they have different colors. (This is important for later.)

Here's something else you should notice from these (2 + 2 + 2 + 2) eight states:

- With 2 of the "positive" emotions, the opposite is a positive
- With 2 of the "positive" emotions, the opposite is a negative
- With 2 of the "negative" emotions, the opposite is a positive
- With 2 of the "negative" emotions, the opposite is a negative

You can have all the knowledge and all the skill in the world, but if your emotions (especially fear) hold you back, if you can't "get over yourself" so to speak ... then you can't do anything!

This is why so many people have trouble putting up an opt-in page, can't YET run a live webinar, and so on. Too many negatives holding you back and not enough positives pushing you forward.

How to Change Your Behavior (The Way That Works)

And I think the reason so many people can't move past it is they either let it take them over, try to ignore it, fight it or even go against it.

You have to REDIRECT it and USE it to your advantage. When I was young, I was in (music) band, played sports and gave school presentations probably like you.

Anytime I "fought" what I was feeling, it distracted me from hitting the baseball. BUT ... if I were nervous about playing saxophone in concert, I would use that alertness to do an even better job than I would otherwise.

(Maybe that explains why I was always stuck in leftfield/shortstop/3rd base in baseball, but was 1st/2nd chair in band class?)

To improve any skill, you need to go from:

- unconscious incompetence (unaware you're doing it wrong), to ...
- conscious incompetence (discover WHAT you're doing wrong), then to ...

- conscious competence (doing it somewhat right even if you have to work at it), and finally ...
- unconscious competence (doing it automatically as easily as breathing or driving a car).

The seven stages of grief (shock, denial, anger, bargaining, guilt, depression, and acceptance) take you up to "conscious competence."

Twelve-step recovery programs (problem, awareness, decision, inventory, admission, readiness, openness, details, repair, inventory, meditation, repetition) stop before you reach "unconscious competence."

Unconscious Incompetence
to Unconscious Competence

I don't know many things, but I DO know about overcoming your fear of public speaking to run webinars because I've done it. And the secret isn't figuring it out at once, it's focusing on ONE problem you have (namely, running one in the first place, slurring your words, stopping for questions, silence or dead air ... slowly fixing things, until one day you realize you don't have to try at all ...

- 0% of the way there: ground zero (not online, not doing webinars)
- 20% of the way there: unconscious incompetence (running your first webinar, just doing "something")
- 40% of the way there: conscious incompetence (aware of little things you're doing wrong on a webinar)

- 60% of the way there: conscious competence (fixing little problems namely, for example, breathing on a webinar)
- 80% of the way there: unconscious competence (running an excellent webinar automatically)

If you've heard of the 80/20 rule, you know that 20% of the effort will bring you 80% of the results.

Life's 80/20 rule applies here in that the last 80% is the hardest ... you can put in just 20% of the effort to achieve an 80% skill level (the beginning of "unconscious competence") ... but now you're running webinars and doing them correctly: making sales, being a good presenter, recording it, all that good stuff.

Let's connect your "skill" (good or bad) your "emotion" (good or bad) ... we want your negative state to be in the past, and your positive state to be in the future, right?

Anger, disgust, fear, and sadness should somehow fit into past – the "unconscious incompetence" and "conscious incompetence" areas.

Anticipation, joy, trust, and surprise are in your future – "conscious competence" and "unconscious competence."

When you're incompetent, you're in a negative state. When you're competent, you're positive. But how do you REACH there?

Why Don't You Go "Confuse" Yourself!

The key is confusing yourself and let me explain. Think about when somebody won you over by making you laugh, overloading you with information or just confusing you with conflicting information until you gave up. You change your state through confusion.

The lack of confusion is also how you stay in a state, and why you're stuck in the state you're in now. Let's see what happens if we pair the "unconscious" states (beginning and end) with emotions NOT opposites, and "conscious" states (middle stages where we're improving) with emotions that ARE opposites – to add the "confusion" factor where we make a change?

The Exact Roadmap to Do It Today

We have this roadmap of going from "guilt" to "love."

- unconscious incompetence = sadness + disgust = guilt
- conscious incompetence = anger + fear (opposites)
- conscious competence = ANTICIPATION + SURPRISE (opposites)
- unconscious competence = JOY + TRUST = love

What you'll do is use fear and anger to rise above the guilt, take some action out of impulse, experience anticipation and surprise once you realize what you're doing, experience the joy of completion and the trust that it's possible to repeat.

Here are the steps you need to go through in order, for example, to become confident with webinars:

Stage 1: Unconscious Incompetence: (sadness + disgust) Do you feel bad because you're not making enough money? Feel guilty because you're not doing enough? It's okay to blame your "past" self for not doing enough … cry it out so you can move past it.

Your present and future self WILL run one webinar this week, it's going to happen.

Stage 2: Conscious Incompetence: (anger + fear) Remember when someone said you weren't good enough to do something? That person would probably say the same about you and webinars. Prove them wrong. Are you jealous of someone else, who has more than you do? It's not fair, you deserve it more than they do! Become mad enough to make a difference.

Maybe you could do a webinar better than "they" would ... now you have something they don't.

Anyway, your marketing message isn't leaving now – you need to run at least ONE webinar. Try it. What you've been doing so far isn't working it ... attack this directly.

Stage 3: Conscious Competence: (ANTICIPATION + SURPRISE) You're allowed to be a "little" bit nervous trying something, such as webinars, that you haven't done before. But one of the cool things about doing a webinar is that you don't know what's going to happen. Doing a webinar means you have to move outside your comfort zone, but what have you got to lose?

The absolute worst thing that happens is that no one shows up, or no one likes your webinar, and guess what ... you're at the same place you are now! In other words, you have nothing to lose and everything to gain. Once you do this you'll know where your limits are.

Stage 4: Unconscious Competence: (JOY + TRUST) You completed the hard part ... that first 2 minutes of the webinar when you were nervous, and you powered through it to the fun part. You finished your first webinar, and you're already excited about doing another. Even if just one person said you were excellent, that made it worthwhile, didn't it? You can't believe it took you this long to run a live webinar like this. You want to do it repeatedly. Your next webinar will be even better.

If you're not ready to run webinars, replace "run a webinar" with "make an opt-in page" … "set up a payment button" … or even "exercising" or "quitting your job" or "dating" …

I'm not saying I know everything about everything, but you can apply what I know about webinar confidence to your life, so you can tackle that problem of having a SKILL but not yet having the CONFIDENCE to put yourself out there.

Part 4: Double Your Income

"Wealth is created in short bursts by positioning yourself in front of massive growth."
– Bill Gates

Chapter 18: Just Plug in the Printer Already

"The successful person has the habit of doing the things failures don't like to do."
– Thomas Edison

I remember my parents yelling me quite a bit growing up. Sometimes it was my fault, sometimes it wasn't. Many times, they were mad at me because I "broke the computer" by "typing and clicking around too fast."

My Dad in particular was good at electronics, building things, fixing them, but when it came to electronics he was obsessed with static electricity and how it could destroy electronics.

In particular, he yelled when I plugged in the computer cables "in the wrong order." Here's what I mean: I was supposed to plug the power cord into the computer LAST. I had to be sure to plug the printer in first, then the keyboard and mouse, then the monitor, then the printer if we had one, but the power cord went in LAST … or I was in big trouble!

In the 6th grade (age 10) we could obtain an old (MS-DOS) computer with WordPerfect on it, to use for class assignments. This was long before we had anything resembling the Internet in the classroom. I remember setting it up with a few my friends after school, and I freaked out when he just began plugging the printer, power, monitor, and all the cables in a seemingly random order.

And guess what … nothing bad happened. The computer turned on, it didn't explode, and static electricity didn't destroy the computer.

The point I'm trying to make is this: too many people are superstitious. They act or pass on bad information just because someone repeated the incorrect information enough times, and maybe even made them SCARED to do otherwise. On the Internet, it's okay to be reckless and make mistakes, because most things you'll be doing, like setting up websites and promoting them, are undoable and redoable.

Let's talk about what you need in place to make money on the Internet. We discussed the "Income Machine" before, all the pieces you need in place to have a consistent income …

Income Machine Reviewed

Someone comes to your website and they read a web page seeing you have something to sell. It's not just "a thing for sale" but it's the SOLUTION to their current problem. Stop having headaches, quit smoking, play the guitar like a rock star, learn Spanish in 7 days, win your ex back, lose man-boob fat, become a grandmaster champion at chess.

They have this desperate need, it's your job to hook them (usually with a BRIEF micro-story about what brought them there and what they're feeling) and present your solution to them in a way that stands out from the competition, usually with implied urgency on why they need this at the moment. We call this a sales letter, I've mentioned this idea earlier in the book and we'll touch on it again. It's that important.

My favorite kind of sales letter is a "direct response" style where it's just a long web page with nothing else to click or do, other than read this message and click the buy button.

Someone clicks and goes to a page where they enter their payment details, I use PayPal.com most of the time for this, free. (They take a small percentage of your sales.)

After paying, they're sent back to your website to grab the thing they just bought. We call this a download page and it might have a video or a downloadable digital PDF report they'll use to solve their problem. We call this a download page.

Sales letter, download page. I made good money for years using only these two components.

As part of the "Income Machine" system, we have you set up a few other things to ensure your income stays RELIABLE instead of FLASH-IN-THE-PAN.

First, a mailing list. Most people don't know about these although sites like Facebook, Amazon.com, Groupon e-mail them weekly if not daily. People voluntarily complete a form and this adds them to a mailing list they can unsubscribe from at any time, with one click. You can have thousands, tens of thousands, hundreds of thousands of people on this list. You have something to say to them, you write one message, click "Send" … and all of them receive the message.

You register at a place like Aweber.com and place one of these sign-up forms on your download page (we call this a "buyer's list) and now if you come out with an update to this information product they just bought, all of them receive a copy of the newest version. You come out with a new product to sell, you can send them to go buy it. You can recommend other people's products and receive a commission. Send them all to comment on your latest blog post. Or reply to give you their testimonial. You have the idea.

We also create what's called a "prospect list" where we create a squeeze page or a forced opt-in page. This is a web page where we offer a gift, something like, "How to Play Guitar in Just 20 Minutes" where you show the BASICS of playing guitar in a quick 5-page report or 10-minute video just starting people, whetting their appetite.

They come to this web page, they see you're offering a free report, you have a couple bullet points explaining what RESULT they'll receive ... they enter in their name and e-mail, they receive the free 5-page report, now they're on your PROSPECT LIST, which they can opt out from at any time.

Then, you create what's called a follow-up sequence where people receive an e-mail from your autoresponder system where you make sure they received the report AND you give them many reasons to buy your full-blown guitar course ... if they saw results from the free report, imagine what they'll receive from the $97 home study course ...

If you want to talk about other subjects related to learning guitar, or you want an Internet presence, you create a blog and post a quick 3-5 minute video monthly, or write a 400-word post yourself, or choose the topic and pay someone $5 on Fiverr.com to write that blog post for you. This way, if someone wants to do a background check on you, they can find all sorts of content with your name on it so they know you know what you're talking about … and if someone stumbles onto that blog from the search engines …it links back to your opt-in page and your sales letter!

Do you have a few extra minutes remaining? Good, you can improve your download page into what's called a membership site – not necessarily a site where you charge monthly, but a site where everyone can log in with their own username and password. (We have a course for this at MembershipCube.com.)

What's wonderful about a membership site is that you can add videos, extra downloads, and more into one easy to navigate site if you decide to add bonuses or expand that download page.

Then Adjust

Then you just add traffic. Start an affiliate program, post articles, forum posts, and more. At that point, you can look at your complete system and decide where your weakness is …

- Is your sales letter not converting? (The answer is yes if you convert at less than 0.1%)
- Is your opt-in page not converting? (The answer is yes if you convert at less than 50%)
- Are you missing a follow-up sequence? (The answer is yes if you don't have at least a daily e-mail for the first 10 days after someone signs up)
- Do you need more traffic to your opt-in page?
- Do you need more traffic to your sales letter?

- Do you need a bigger list?
- Do you need an upsell? (such as a coaching program)

I know what you're thinking. But I've HEARD of these things, Robert! But do you actually have all these things in place? Do you have an upsell? Do you have a follow-up sequence? Do you know your conversion rate? Is your list big enough? If the answer to any of those is "no" … then DO IT!

Why am I fixating on these "Income Machine" fundamentals? Think about what a basketball coach or golf coach would do … (watch some movies like "The Mighty Ducks" or "Coach Carter" or "Rudy" or even "Space Jam" if you don't know the answer).

Answer: The fundamentals … shoot the basketball in the hoop 500 times in a row … swing that golf swing and look at a photograph to correct the hip or elbow stance. When I played Little League the coach would hit grounders, grounders, grounders … fly ball, fly ball, fly ball … line drive, line drive, line drive, until we had the fundamentals down.

Far too many people would rather ignore the fundamentals and focus on the "cutting-edge techniques" … treating something like "joining a traffic exchange" the end-all-be-all of Internet marketing, when it's just a small "trick" that you can file into the "traffic" category. Or a "1 dollar trial", which you can file into the "sales letter" category. Or how about article marketing, which you can file into the "traffic" or even the "blogging" category.

If you don't have the entire Income Machine set up, the way to increase your income is to set up each of those pieces: niche and domain name, web host, opt-in page, follow-up sequence, blog, sales letter, membership site, download page.

If have all those pieces in place (including the follow-up sequence, let's be honest) then you need to identify the weak point in that system. It might be conversion for you (if you send 1000 clicks and don't make 5-10 sales at an under-$97 price). Once you have a critique from a copywriter and fix it, you need traffic, which leads to a bigger list, which in turn should solve all if not most of your problems.

Let's look at a few useful quotes before we move on …

- "Sell the sizzle not the steak." – Elmer Wheeler
- "The secret to getting everything you want is helping others get what they want." – Zig Ziglar
- "Pioneers get arrowed in the back." – Dan Kennedy

The biggest problem I see people have when they're selling their products: being too in love with that product. They care too much that it took "them" 20 hours or 2 years to create it. Or that it contains 15 hours. Or that the book is 400 pages long. If you're trying to sell this thing to me, I only care about what it does for me. What's the OUTCOME? Not what you know, not what I can learn, but what IT can do FOR ME.

Don't worry about holding back "just one thing" from your free content, sales letter, or book, in the hopes that I'll buy your upsell or bonus DVD course. Just show me how to solve this simple problem and if you have an upsell, it solves the NEXT LOGICAL PROBLEM, not this same problem that I still haven't solved.

And, finally, to explain that Dan Kennedy quote, don't try to "innovate." If you try to innovate you'll either try to make something work that just won't (think about things that never caught on like the Segway or RadioShack's CueCat) or you have the right thing but your timing is wrong (like tablets ... didn't sell well in one decade but were a hit in another). Instead, look at what's being taught poorly in the marketplace. Look at the problems real people have where you can solve it better than anyone else.

Chapter 19: Strategy versus Tactics (How to Give Yourself an Instant Pay Raise WITHOUT Resorting to Cheap Gimmicks!)

"People don't want quarter-inch drills.
They want quarter-inch holes."
– Theodore Levitt

I thought I was so clever. Back when I was a teenager, I had what I thought was a wonderful idea ... write an e-book teaching how to program PHP scripts for web pages, load a batch of tools onto a "three inch CD" for 20 dollars and sell a million copies.

Have you seen those 3-inch CD's? Basically, when you load a CD onto the CD tray, there's a smaller "indent" where a smaller CD fits. Here's where I thought had hit the jackpot: a three inch CD would fit into a standard sized envelope and would mail with just one stamp.

There's only a few gaping flaws with that line of thinking and that's ...

- People weren't going to buy my product "just" because it's on a CD
- That time I "might" have spent burning CD's and mailing them would be better spent: improving the product, the copy, the advertising, even making more products
- Delivering a "real" product, digitally, with an instant download, would take zero time, with zero cost, and customers would receive the product instantly after buying

My mentor at the time (Teresa King) told me to test the product online first. If it sold well and people were actually ASKING for a physical version, and were willing to pay more to justify the cost, then it would be a hit ...

What's the moral of the story? Mailing a product on a disk isn't a business model, and it's probably the LAST thing you should think about ... only after a product is already selling, and even then, that's one of those little "gimmicks" you add to earn a 1% or 2% boost to your profits. It's a TACTIC, not a STRATEGY.

Be careful about relying on too many tactics to make money. You'll market yourself into a corner and wonder where it went wrong, and here's why ...

Superstitious Marketing!

Has anyone given you "weird" marketing advice like this?

- Always price your products ending in "7" ... like 27, 49, and 97!
- Always put the text "Add to Cart" on your order buttons
- Always have an orange order button and nothing else
- Only e-mail your list once per week
- Run a "dime sale"
- Don't ever launch a product unless you have testimonials

Here's what happened: someone had a successful sales letter and a winning product, so they decided to run some split tests ... send half their traffic to the $17 price, half to the $19.95 price. Half their traffic to the blue order button, half to the orange order button.

These gurus have given you a list of "best practices" to put onto your website so you don't have to start from scratch. Have this white background. Use that red headline. Place your testimonials in little blue boxes.

What's the problem? Poor misguided newbies (and not-so-newbies) see this list of best practices and think ... if I make sure my video auto plays on this web page, if I have a 30-day guarantee ... then I can put any old piece of crap on the market, and it will sell!

Can I told you what I did years ago to dramatically boost my product sales?

- I limited the number of digital copies of my product I was selling ... and it worked ONCE!
- I warned about (then increased) the price of my product ... and it worked ONCE!
- I increased the price with every sale ... and it worked ONCE!
- I added a countdown timer ... and it worked ONCE!

These tactics boosted sales, but they weren't the ONLY reason I made sales. It enhanced something already selling (mostly by making it novel and newsworthy). If you distribute a bad product that doesn't work, or no one wants it, or no one needs it, then these gimmicks won't help you. And even if they do, they only work once or twice before your audience becomes used to it and you have to think of a new gimmick.

Could your webinar convert better? Is your sales letter not selling? Here's an idea ... learn to sell THE FUNDAMENTALS.

Why Your Sales Letter Isn't Selling

I can look at most sales letters and in seconds, notice at least 10 BASIC things that hurt sales. Fix them and you'll notice an improvement, keep those things in mind for your next launch and it'll pay repeatedly …

1. Is your headline interesting enough to pull me in and make me to keep reading your web page?
2. Do you identify the problem that brought me to your web page, align with my values, then transition into the solution, your product?
3. Do you CLEARLY introduce your product and only ask for the sale once you've explained what it is? (once you're "earned the right to sell to me")
4. Can you find large chunks of text that you need to break into smaller paragraphs, add bullet points, headlines, and graphics to make it easier to read?
5. Is your copy "story heavy" (too much story before introducing the offer) or "offer heavy"? (explaining the offer without building its importance up first)
6. Do you have several links and buttons on the page that your visitors can click that drops them into your order form area?
7. Do you have an offer stack where you list all the components of your course in one place, building up the total value, then revealing the low price?
8. Do you clearly explain what price people will pay? (don't make them click through to discover, just freaking tell them)

Do you see what I mean? Basic things that will help you much more than running an automated webinar, adding a countdown timer, ending your price in $9.99. You'll actually make improvements to your web page that make sense.

If you want to add your picture to that sales letter, it's up to you. If you want to add a logo, I would, and it's increased conversions, but it's up to you. Giant red headline with quotes around it? Be my guest.

An auto play audio button has always given me a tiny conversion boost. A graphic representation like a 3D cover or 3D box would be awesome … but a polished turd is still a turd!

It's not just sales letters. I once attended a webinar where the presenter was inexperienced, nervous, afraid to sell at the end, messed everything up by offering a Q&A session at the end, and lasting for 3 hours when 1 hour would have done the job.

You could tell by his energy level on the call, and by his e-mail follow-up sequence afterward, that the webinar didn't sell. Instead of figuring out WHY it didn't sell (strategy), he resorted to the gimmicks (tactics) and spent a week editing the recording to remove all the "umm's", discounted the price, made every mistake and still wondered why it didn't sell.

Real Live Case Studies to Back It Up

I can think back to story after story where … we were selling a 4-module course on WordPress that wasn't selling, I recorded a 12-minute video in the middle of the night showing one plugin part of the course, and woke with more than $16,000 in PayPal the next morning ... because I discovered what the marketplace was demanding, and adjusted my marketing so it made it clear that I was the one to give it to them ...

Years ago, Lance and I launched a course on membership sites that we thought wouldn't sell. We were hoping for ten to twenty thousand dollars in sales over a 2 week period. The marketplace wanted a "drip content" plugin at the time, that was our positioning, and BOOM! More than 35,000 in sales in the first 5 hours ...

And another time, we launched our outsourcing course explaining how at the time, I'd had over 1.3 million words (something like 150 hours) of audio turned into articles, reports, products, and books. The problem? No one cares about YOUR 1.3 million words, and no one is ASKING to have 1.3 million words transcribed. Instead, we switched it to a short PowerPoint video demonstrating how if anyone had just 3 minutes, they could create an article, chapter, or blog post. Finally, something people needed, wanted, were asking for, willing to pay money for, that was powerful, easy, and fast, that we could provide.

Would we have turned any of those launches around by adding a "FAQ section" or a countdown timer? Without actually fixing the REAL problem? I doubt it.

Chapter 20: Sell Anything Online Using the Magic of Copywriting

"Watch your thoughts, they become words.
Watch your words, they become actions.
Watch your actions, they become habits.
Watch your habits, they become character.
Watch your character, it becomes your destiny."
– Lao-Tze

We're going to talk today about how to use your words to sell. How to sit, create a simple, a short web page, video, webinar that can do every kind of thing, and receive money from it.

Figure out how to present something in a way that makes people excited, that promises them a result, shows them some amazing results of your own, has them salivating at the mouth to hand over their money to you, to buy into your product, your course, your report, receive your video training, receive your print book, comment on your blog post. It becomes way easier when you apply a system that anyone can use.

I don't know whether you've heard in the past, people saying that they have this confusing, complicated, artsy-fartsy writing process. We're going to throw all that out the window today. I'm going to share with you my special system for enticing people to pay you money from your writing without you having to spend too much effort or time at all writing, without you having to write much either.

Copywriting, Sales Letters, and Persuasion!

I have a few questions for you. Number one, are you willing to do anything that it takes to have the best life possible for you and the best life possible for everyone around you? I hope so.

Now, my other question is, are you putting your best foot forward? What I mean by that is, let's say that, I'm going to assume that you have been to a job interview in the past. You had to give them a piece of paper, call it a résumé. This is a standardized kind of thing where you list what you know, what you do, qualifications, experience, and education.

But you don't make it boring, do you? You try to present yourself as the best version of yourself possible. You'll list your previous employers. You'll say, "Here are the things I've done in the past." You dress up your job qualifications, don't you?

You didn't work at Subway, you were a sandwich engineer. You weren't just a computer programmer at this other job, you were a systems analyst.

In that line of thinking, many of us, when we create websites, web pages on the Internet, we don't make it as exciting as it possibly could be. How do you make things fun and exciting? I'll tell you at once. Think about what results are you telling people.

Let me think of a few courses that we might have for sale. For example, let me list out, we have a course on webinars, we have a course on how to write articles. Just so I'm not limited to my little area, let's say that you might have some course on real estate flipping, another course on self-help. Let's give a list of different scenarios.

I've listed on a piece of paper – webinars, articles, real estate, and self-help. These are all things you might have for sale online. If we were not even trying and I was telling you, "I have this course that shows you how to run webinars – the technical stuff, the confident stuff, how to be a presenter, all that fun stuff, how to create a product or pitch a course live on the Internet." How would I present that?

If you weren't thinking that much about it, you would say, "I'm going to show you the technical details. I'm going to share with you the best practices on how to talk to a thousand people."

Let's think about this for a second … webinars, how to talk to a thousand people. Half the battle, when being a good marketer online and copywriting, is you think, "What holes can I poke in that marketing there?" I talk about webinars, I say you can talk to a thousand people on the Internet.

If you have a book that you just published, you want some copies, talk to a thousand people, and achieve some sales. If you have a product you just published, like an e-book or a video course, talk to a thousand people. Sounds great, except the hole we can poke in that is now scary. Now you've turned it into public speaking.

You tell me a thousand people. I'm telling you, a thousand people is terrifying. What's a better way? A better way is for you to run a webinar, now what happens? What is the result of running that webinar? Off the top of my head, instant sales.

Off the top of my head is that you can sit at your computer, it's less work than writing – you don't have to write anything. You appear on a webinar, you hit the button, you start talking, and you present something. You can refine your sales pitch if you do, at some point, want to be a speaker because you might realize that we're going to target people who want to be speakers, people who are coaches, who are authors.

We said, "In the past, you've had to circulate and present yourself on radio shows, speak on various stages, but now you can do this thing called a webinar, stay home, and run these from home. If you want to connect with someone new, instead of having to go to their event, instead of having to call them on the phone, have them promote a link to their subscribers, present on your webinar, and now it's even better than a radio interview, or a Skype interview, or even a recorded audio because it's live. People can see your screen and you can make it as simple or as complex as you want."

You can poll the audience. You can follow-up with them afterward. You can have someone else answering the chat box. If you want to be the speaker, if you want to present your thing, you can ignore that chat box and have an assistant respond for you. Webinars, instant sales, if you can pick up the phone, you can make money.

Now, articles, let's think about that. This thing called an article that means that you can write a 400-word, about two-thirds of a page, lesson. You can submit an article to various sites, this gives you links back to your site.

If we're thinking about articles, if you weren't thinking again, you might write or you might say, "Articles means you can make money as a writer." Now, poke holes now, what's the problem with that? If I say make money as a writer, what comes to your mind? You can be a ghostwriter – spend a year writing someone else's book that they receive credit for. You are paid maybe $5,000 for a year of work.

Writing makes people think of being up late at night, typing on the computer, editing sentences, checking spelling, checking grammar, terrible. Articles, how do we make articles sexy? How we make articles fun?

The way to make things fun – I am making this up as I go along – is to give people big results, or to save people time, or maybe make things simple I guess, if I had to choose a third. But the point of copywriting is to give people something new, give people something newsworthy.

Anytime that we can break the mold, or we can have a system where – in this niche in the past – people were used to this downside of it. Webinars' downside, public speaking. Articles' downside is work, writing, time. If we can take something like writing articles, reduce the work, the aggravation, the time, now we're talking. Low hanging fruit, easy answer is make an article in X minutes.

Actually, I can show anyone how to make an article in less than three minutes – that's if they take a while on it. I can show people how to make a hundred articles in six hours. Do you want to know what it is? There's a particular system.

Systems

There's a particular set of steps to follow. Every article I write is written in the same way. The titles are written in the same way. The body, the number of sentences, paragraphs, the words I use, and it's all systematic. It's done in a way where I've written enough, I'd looked at enough articles to notice a pattern.

With the product, selling my pattern, my system, my workflow, you just follow the steps. You don't have to think because thinking is what normally hampers your writing. If I can show you how to take something that used to take you an hour, an article, do it in three minutes, now what's that worth to you?

Sometimes, we can't remove a problem. We have to do what a smart guy named Joe Sugarman does – acknowledge the shortcomings, but explain them away.

An article, yes, you have to do some writing and you can't circumvent the choice that either you have to write an article, or someone else does. If someone else writes it, it's obviously not going to be as good as if you'd made it. You will have to pay them money. But let's maybe reduce that as much as possible.

We have a product called MakeAProduct.com – funny how it's a product, I'll make a product anyway – it's a membership site. It shares our system of speaking out articles with another system of transcribing it. Normally, what many people will do, if we were trying to think of a sales letter because I am leading to a point here but I'm explaining to you, when I first approach how I'm going to sell something, I don't start thinking about what's the first sentence? What's the headline?

I start thinking about, "What are we trying to say? What kind of offer are we presenting?" Based on the niche or that problem, if someone's coming to us trying to figure whether they know they want articles made, what's in their mind? What's their current problem? What assumptions are they already making?

With articles, they're already assuming there's some work involved. But if we can show them how to do it faster, maybe they won't mind they work. Let's try to explain away the various difficulties with articles. We list a couple, we've got writer's block, time, energy, and we've got results.

Maybe we'll make a sales letter where, if all we do is we think about what are these objections and we take care of them, take people past them, through them, or explain them away so they don't matter, we've done all the selling we need. All that's left is explaining what's in our offer, what's in our package.

People come to us because they have this problem where writing articles takes too long, it's too hard, they're not consistent – I'll even write that. Whenever I'm writing an article, I'm thinking, "What are the top four objections? What's the most appropriate order in which to answer them?" because if we're, I don't want to say clever but, if we're careful, we can actually answer these four objections in a way that explains the problem at the same time, or explains the problem and explains the solutions.

Here's what I mean. We have a product about writing an article, but we can't assume that everyone in the world knows exactly what we're talking about, can we? We can assume a little – we can assume people know that we have a set about writing. But maybe they didn't know that, from creating one article, you could potentially receive a thousand clicks, a thousand subscribers. They don't know that, if you had a blog and you posted to it once per day, that's a new web page that can be listed under Google, tweeted out, liked, favorited, shared, syndicated to other sites – that's one objection.

One objection might be, "It's not worth my time to create an article." To answer that, look at all the various ways that you can use one article to build traffic. On top of that, now we're using the article as a credibility tool to now become a recognized author.

Objection number one is the results – maybe show a few screenshots of your best article. If you published a hundred articles, the top five of those are going to be well performing. Now, I know from experience, the problem is you don't know which five until you publish them, but that's also something where you can differentiate yourself, at least what I do.

I know many people who can only write five articles in a year. They worry about all the social media this, Panda that, PageRank this other stuff. They have this confusing system that no one understands, including them. It returns to, we've talked in the previous episodes about having a business versus having a hobby.

Just dabbling, writing an article here and there for fun, that's a hobby. But being able to do it in three minutes, publishing an article a day, monthly? Now that's consistent traffic, consistent lead generation, you're consistently putting your brand out there. If could show you how to make an article in three minutes, do it thirty times a month.

Let's say you did one a day – this is coming together – three minutes a day, give me three minutes a day, I'll give you 90 articles, 900 backlinks, 1,800 subscribers, and you can repeat it as much as you want. Now we're moving into something cool.

One thing I want to mention – which we'll return to but I want you to be aware of it – is this idea of writing from a template because writing isn't fun. But this whole thing we're doing where we're thinking about our strategy, assembling pieces, moving the blocks around so it's like this well-crafted argument, that's kind of fun.

What helps us are these various templates. I mentioned one, it's this if-then kind of thing. If you can make a statement, what we're going to be talking about in a few minutes, are headlines because headlines are so much fun. A buddy of mine who's a copywriter, Steven Schwartzman, used to have a service called Mr. Headline – I want to say it was $97.00.

For $97.00 he'd write your headline. How cool a job is that? That's some Don Draper level skill. You are paid a hundred dollars, fart around for about an hour, thinking about all this crazy stuff, and he'd give you a few headlines. But that's barely writing.

He would write 50 words for a hundred dollars, two dollars per word. I'll take that all freaking day long. To give you an idea of Mr. Headline, I'm going to pull up — I mentioned this in the last call – Sales Page Tactics. I think he wrote it for Sales Page Tactics Volume 2, the headline he wrote for me was ...

"If You're Not Using These Advanced Sales Page Tactics,
You Might As Well Throw $10.00 In The Trash Every Time
Someone Visits Your Web Page!"

This is called an if-then statement. In programming, we use it a lot. Funny how my knowledge in programming applies to other areas, funny how I'm a computer programmer but copywriting is so much fun because we're not trying to be literary snobs. We're not trying to be Jack London or anything. We're just trying to distribute some words that sell.

Modeling

What's so funny about copywriting is that you can look at someone else's web page, if you look at it in the right way, you can say, and

"What is it about that statement that got me to keep reading or got me to buy? I'm going to not copy it but maybe model it." A good way to explain this entire call is this thing called modeling.

Think about it. If you visited Facebook's front page today, if someone covered the logo, you'd still know it's Facebook's website, wouldn't you? If you went to Amazon.com's website and somebody covered Amazon.com, you went to eBay, Craigslist, you'd know where you were. If not, you'd say, "This is a Craigslist knock-off. This is an Amazon knockoff."

Particular things look a particular way. If you went to Internet Marketer's website and it was a piece of paper, you'd say, "This is the Internet Marketing website." If you went to a WordPress site with the web page as a full-width design, there's maybe several columns, videos, different pictures, you'd say, "It's probably a WordPress kind of site, or something selling software, or a plug-in."

Different things look a particular way as when we're talking about writing, particular things are written in a particular way. People who tried all kinds of variations, if you follow what works, you're 80% of the way there.

If you have a white background, a headline that's red, with quotes around it, now you're almost there. All you have to do is put some words there. This whole thing about modeling, why are we even at the wheel when we have something that works?

Headlines

If-then statement, super-great, super-strong headline if you have the right one because, if you can convince that something is easy, you can then promise a result, but because you're mixing these around, it's not obvious to the typical person.

We say, "If you're not using these advanced sales page tactics, you might as well throw $10.00 in the trash every time someone visits your sales page." We could have said, "These tools will give you more money." But it's more dramatic to say, in this case, that if you don't have these things, you're losing money.

Another way we can use the if-then statement is, if you can do this then you can do that. A few minutes ago I said, "If you can talk on the phone, you could present on a webinar." We can pick something that's easy, that anyone can agree that they can do, that they've probably done today already, then we'll promise them this big result – funny how that works.

Another easy headline formula is ask a question. The easiest kind of question to ask is a "what-if" question and a "who-else-wants-to" because these are the headlines you see everywhere. But there's a reason that the clichés work.

Question, what if I could show you a way to sit at your computer for three minutes and create an article that is spread around a hundred different places on the Internet? That's cool, right? We're not necessarily promising a million dollars. My business partner Lance Tamashiro, love to give that guy shout-outs, props, his first course said something like, "If you have 14 minutes, I will show you how to receive 134 leads in your e-mail marketing system." That also brought in the time component. He said, "I'm going to give you 134 leads," but it only takes 14 minutes.

It's kind of going counter. At the time, this thing called list building was a huge niche to enter. There were many hype-y sales letters saying, "All you have to do is push one button and you'll have 20,000 subscribers falling over themselves to throw their wallets at you," that kind of thing.

People would promise a million subscribers, there would be courses on how to receive a hundred thousand subscribers from scratch in 7 days. He didn't know how to show that. He didn't know how to receive a hundred thousand subscribers in 7 days. Even the guy selling the courses didn't know that. They were going too far, I think.

He went the opposite way – not the opposite way, he didn't say, "Oh, list building sucks. It's so much hard work." He said you make a small result, but notice, he also set a short time. He said, "134 leads in 14 minutes." My immediate thought there was, "Yes, but I could put in another 14 minutes repeatedly and receive thousands of subscribers, receive what I want anyway."

We don't want to become too clever, but if we can look at when I saw this person's headline, I don't want to just grab it and change out one word. Maybe I'll grab it, figure out what they were trying to achieve, and use it in this other way. It was if-then, there's the what-if, and maybe if he was writing some headlines, he can say, "What if I could hand-deliver 134 subscribers to you?"

Another thing I want to mention because we're throwing these out there, it's not a required, but if you can show people things, or make them visualize it, or use action words, all the better. The funny thing about copywriting, especially for sales letters for the Internet is, the more basic you can make your wordage, the better.

If you can say things instead of saying, "I want you to achieve this number of subscribers," "Can I give this to you?" "Can I hand this to you?" "Have you ever been so frustrated trying to build a list that you just threw up your hands in frustration, shake your head, can't reach it, and you're tired?" See what I mean?

You don't want to become too involved in storytelling, but give people something to imagine. Many times, I'll be grammatically incorrect sometimes. I'll even start a sentence in the present tense and end it in the past tense. I might say something like, "Here's where you are at the moment. You want your own freedom, your own business, and you know that you need a website. Wouldn't it be wonderful if I gave you a website right away and now you have it built up, ready to go, and making money?"

See what I did there? It's grammatically incorrect if you want to be an English snob. But we want to make money instead! It's funny how copywriting, short sentences, fourth-grade reading level, move straight to the point, active sentences, short sentences, short words, powerful words – these are all things that help you.

Who Else Wants to …?

We'll be talking about headlines in a minute. I guess you can have an if-then statement. Ask a question like, "What if I do this?" Who else wants to _____?

When we run split tests, which means that we'll see how one web page converts, how one web page converts sales and opt-ins versus another, every time we try "who else wants to?" and promise a big result, it usually wins.

Why is that? Because, when you say, "who else wants to?" that phrasing forces you to punch up the benefits. Again, we're not saying a million subscribers, but we want to list who else wants this. Who else wants to does a few things.

First, who else means that I've already shown someone else how to do this because it's as if you say, "Who else wants ice cream?" it sounds as though I've already given someone ice cream, someone else receives ice cream. Who else wants to build a subscriber list? Or who else wants to add 134 new e-mail subscribers from 14 minutes of punching a button, or 14 minutes of effort.

I don't like to use the word "work" – I'll explain that in a short while – but when we say, "who else wants to?" we have to put in results and there's an implied social proof. Anytime you can imply something and make people come to the wrong conclusions, it becomes much more reinforced, I guess I should say.

You imply something, if they don't understand it, that's weaker. But if you can suggest something, just by reading "who else wants to?" now they understand I'm not the first, now that makes sense.

Who else wants to build a list of 134 subscribers in 14 minutes? Now, another enhancer to this – this isn't the whole headline on its own but – if you can list three things, or sometimes I'll do three results, or three problems and three solutions.

Here's what I mean. Who else wants to build an e-mail subscriber list? All right, that's fine. Who else wants to build an e-mail subscriber list, or who else wants to add 187 leads? That's fine also. But if you had to list three things – it could either be one thing leads to the next, leads to the next.

It could be who's coming to our web page and what do they want? Because some people come to our web page, they know they want e-mail subscribers. Some people don't know that. Some people, they just want to reach the point, they say, "E-mail subscribers are wonderful, but what I want are some sales, what I want are some clicks." There's our three – subscribers, clicks, and sales.

If we can say, "Who else wants 187 new subscribers, as many clicks on your web page as you want, and to double your sales by next week?" That's off the top of my head but that's cool how, by plugging in a formula, even something that you thought of off the top of your head is kind of cool.

Headlines Continued ...

We talked about webinars, articles, how about real estate? Real estate's exciting because with real estate, I know people who can put in six hours of work – most of that's on the contracts – and walk off with $12,000 in commission.

With real estate, I don't know that much about real estate so we won't go into as much detail as with webinars and articles, but going into real estate, you might be thinking, "What are people thinking about real estate?"

"Will the bubbles burst?" The bubble bursts every ten years. The realest things like real estate, when that's at the peak, any idiot can make money from real estate sitting at a desk. But when things are dipping, maybe you have to use someone else's strategy.

With something like real estate, you have to have something unique and different, have your own little system. Maybe it's house flipping, or maybe it's some technical thing, and show current testimonials because there's no point in having testimonials about real estate if they're from three years ago before the bubble burst.

It's always the same process. We go into real estate with our real-estate product. We're thinking, "What are the four assumptions people are making about real estate or about a particular method or a particular course about making through real estate?" We develop those new particular objections.

People might have a vague idea. Maybe they'll think about real estate, that it doesn't work whatsoever, you end by risking a wad of money as far as paying the taxes, or being stuck with a house you can't sell, or being stuck with the renters from hell, things like that.

You go into thinking about what are the objections then we turn that into, "Now, what are we going to promise?" That leads me to, what's your offer? What are you offering someone?

The Promise

It doesn't have to be 50 hours of videos. It doesn't have to be 50 DVDs. But what's your impressive package? I'll list a couple out for you. We have a course called Membership Cube, teaches you how to set up a membership site throughout, how to have paying members, how to drip content, how to create a community, how to entice people to participate.

Membership Cube, there's all that training. In our sales letter for that, we list out the various modules. There's a training part of it, then there's the membership software. What makes us unique is that usually, when you're trying to make a membership site, you can buy the software itself – usually the training sucks – or you can buy someone else's training, but you have to go ahead, and buy the software. But what we've done is we found the best membership plug-in on the market and we've bought it for you.

It's a one-shot deal, no hidden fees, you just receive that. There's the training, there's the membership software, we have various plug-ins that we've built on top of this to improve it. I guess I would say that's our entire offer. I could go into detail about what the different plug-ins do, become technical about that, why the membership software itself is the best, and why our training's the best. But that is our offer.

If you were smart about sending resumes back when you were working a job or if you're still working a job, you tailored your resume towards the person to whom you're applying for.

For example, I had a friend in college, when he would apply to a "database engineer" position, he would emphasize his database experience, his training, his school and all that. When he was applying to a Microsoft or an Oracle kind of job where they hired him for his knowledge of how to use Microsoft SQL Server or Microsoft Windows Server or something, he would emphasize that part of the education.

Just as we noticed who's coming to our site, what do they want? Like how, when I'm teaching computer programming, I'm not selling to the nerd, I'm selling to the marketers. That's who I decided to target.

How we finished with Membership Cube is basically, you can have your membership site online and make money tonight, which I think differs from everyone else, because, for some reason, they try to make it too complicated. That doesn't apply to every niche, but in that one, when I see my competitors, although I don't call them competitors, when I see people in the same niche as mine, I see when they do, I poke holes in what they've done, and I do a better job of marketing to them.

I say, "Here's what the objections are. Here's what my offer is. My offer is that I know your objections are that, instead of making a membership site, it's technical, it's hard work, and it takes you months and months. I'm saying it set up tonight because everything is all in one place – the software, the training, we make it super-simple for you, now it's all set up and online. From there, you can take your baby steps, make it bigger and better. We've prioritized the different tasks you have to do.

That first night, you do the bare bones. You do the minimum to take payments or make money today. Worry about the fancy elements later because you can still use it but it comes later. That's how we take objections, show our offer, and at that point, your sales letter kind of writes itself.

Chapter 21: AIDA Formula

"It's not the daily increase but daily decrease.
Hack away at the unessential."
– Bruce Lee

The formula we're going to use for all copywriting – heck, any writing, including blog posts and e-mails – is AIDA – Attention, Interest, Desire, Action. This is going to be the most important formula, if you don't know it, for everything because this applies to writing reports, this applies to writing blog posts, it applies to writing sales letters, videos, webinars, AIDA – Attention, Interest, Desire, Action.

Here's what it means. Attention means that we have this thing called a headline. We attract someone's attention because, if we just started talking, telling the story, we haven't earned the right yet, have we? I always forget this number but the typical person clicks a web page in a matter of seconds, it's like less than five seconds.

That's fine. That's the universe we live in. Those are the rules we have to follow. If someone on average clicks off in three seconds, let's say, we've devised a way to keep them on for 30 more seconds.

We have this attention-grabbing headline. Usually, it promises something. We have to know our audience to know how crazy we want to make it, how crazy a claim, the normal claims who want to make this.

In Lance's case, what he was going for was that everyone had already heard the usual stuff. His prospects were educated already.

They'd already heard the hype, let's say, or the overhype, or maybe they'd taken some of those courses. He doesn't want to bad-mouth those other courses, but he wants to say, "Hey, look at me, I'm different. Hey, look at me, I'm not saying everything sucks, but I'm more down to earth. Maybe faster than those other guys."

Attention, we have a cool headline that usually prompts crazy results, which might be big results, might be less work, less time – those are the big ones. Headline makes people to read for 30 more seconds.

Now we've gone from three seconds to 30 seconds, but is that enough time for someone to read the whole web page, sales letter, buy from us? Heck no.

We've bought ourselves 30 seconds, how do we buy ourselves three minutes? That's where the Interest comes. We said Attention, Interest, Desire, Action.

Attention = Problem/Story

An attention-grabbing headline is half a sentence. "What if I were to show you how to add 134 leads to your e-mail list in 14 minutes?" We've already identified with the person. They already know what an e-mail subscriber list is, probably. They already know that 134 leads is something worth paying attention to – it's not a lot, but it's a noticeable amount.

That's good, but we need more information. That's where the Interest comes in. If we were to come out and say, "Buy my stuff," it's not going to work. I don't have enough information. If we were going to say, "Here's what's in my course," that's on the right track, but you jumped ahead, haven't you?

When you reach a page that says, "Here, buy my stuff," you're not there yet. You need to "buy them dinner first," that's where we relate to the prospect. We share what their problem is and we assure them that we understand their problem. For me, Interest is where all those objections come into play.

You take those top four objections, arrange them in the right sequence, and that's where we can relate to their problems. List building, let's think about that. Building an e-mail subscriber list, what are the problems?

The problems are similar to membership sites. There's the technical problems, you don't know how to set it up. There's the traffic, people don't know how to entice people to their opt-in page. There's the monetizing, once they're on the list, they don't know how to make money from that.

Actually, if I were to improve Lance's headline at all about 134 leads, I'd also relate how much money that made, except I'd have to try it – I might try it and hate it because, if you made $500.00 in 14 minutes, that's actually kind of cool. Maybe if he made 194 leads and he even made that money over time, he did the work in 14 minutes. It's a gray area, but because he put in 14 minutes of work, although that $500.00 took a year to play out from those particular subscribers, he didn't have to do anything else. It played out on its own.

There's technology, there's making people reach it, monetizing it, and maybe even making the web page to convert. If you have people come to your opt-in page and no one subscribes, you're wasting your money.

There we go – technology, traffic, conversion, and monetization. I would state each of those objections as a question and answer those questions. It's up to you to figure out what's the best order to list those in. I would actually say, it would be technology, traffic, conversion, and monetization.

We can really relate to someone who needs to build a list because we can say, "You know what? I used to be like you. I wanted to make more money on the Internet, I had a website that everyone needed to see. The problem was, no one was there to see it. What I decided to do was build a list, I heard that was an excellent way to have traffic on demand, I could have 10,000, 100,000 people, send that one message and have everyone to show up."

"Great, then I had so many problems. I didn't know what autoresponder service to use. I didn't have a template. I didn't know how it will also look. I didn't know how to redirect someone. I didn't know how to make everything work together."

"I was frustrated by the technical problems. After plenty of guess and check, I finally had a basic web page online, but I didn't know how to entice people to come and see it first. I figured, if people showed up that they'd all register, but how do I make people come to this web page first." There's the traffic part.

"The conversion, eventually, through several steps, I could have 10,000 people come to this web page over time. The problem is, no one signed up. I didn't know why, I didn't know what to fix. I didn't even know where to go from there. Even once they got on my list, I didn't know how to make money from that until I discovered this system. It's a system where," and we go from there.

Interest = Problem/Objections

The Interest is where we state a problem. If we can use the person's top four objections, that means we relate to them. If we order those four objections into a logical systematic sequence – it's usually the simplest to the most difficult, or the objections they'd receive early on, maybe they'd solve that objection and receive another problem.

Maybe they don't even know how to set up a web page. Now that it's set up, now no one's seeing it. Now people see it, now no one's subscribing. Now people are in it, but now it's not making money. We arrange those four objections, now we make a story.

The story I told you was, "I was like you, blah blah blah," you can tell a story like that. You don't have to always tell a story where you were broke. You don't have to start broke. You can tell a story where you came across this problem, or one of your coaching students came across a particular problem, or maybe you're saying, "I know that you have this thing, you have this thing."

We're weaving a story that sets up the problem. You notice how, at the end, I couldn't help but finish that story. The story ends with what your product is. We said, "I'm building a list, building up to this, this, this, this, the answer is Ultimate List Building System." That's the desire part.

Desire = Solution/Product

You move into Desire, now you can't help but explain what the course shows people, what's in the course. This is where we start.

One thing that took me years to figure out is to introduce your product with a bang. We start, attention-grabbing headline, story,

story, story, objection, objection, objection, and we go boom! Here it is. We have it in giant letters.

If you have a logo, if you have a picture of it, boom, there it is – like the song says. Say what your product is. From there, you explain what it is on a big level. Ultimate List Building System gives you everything you need to go from nothing to something that brings you 184 leads every 14 minutes like clockwork. We're going to give you everything – we're going to give you the templates, we're going to tell you what to say, how to do it, give you some e-mail swipe copy.

In this area, we're explaining on a high level what the whole product is. Is that enough? Can we say all that and say bye now? We could, but it'll help us more if, after that point, we analyze the different modules.

Desire, solution/product phase, introduce the product, explain what's in it on a high level, and analyze the various pieces. When I was first selling products on the Internet, I noticed so many web pages where you couldn't even tell what it was.

I don't know whether you've seen videos where someone says, "You don't deserve to be on this page. I'm going to give you a solution. I'm not going to tell you what it is but you push a button, every time you push a button, you receive a thousand dollars. Run it six times a day, you receive $6,000 a day." Have you seen these kinds of videos? You have no idea what it is. Usually it's a piece of crap software that finds domain names, or something similar, or finds affiliate programs.

Back to the point, somebody thinks you don't change on the Internet. One thing that hasn't changed is, a lot of web pages, I can't even tell what they're selling – I don't know whether it's an e-book, video course, DVDs, membership site – even then, what's Module 3 of this course? Why is Module 3 between Modules 2 and 4? Why is that a logical systematic sequence? Are you throwing some stuff at me?

The point of information products is the how-to. Someone's at Point A, they can't play the guitar, you want to move them to Point B – they can play ten songs on the guitar. But to move from Point A to Point B, they need to go through certain modules, certain steps. You usually need four steps or eight steps.

If there's a logical systematic sequence where, if someone's learning the guitar, first they need to learn chords, or maybe they need to learn rhythm or something similar. It makes sense for one to come before the other. You'll be able to justify why your course has all the pieces that it does.

Bucket Brigade

Not only that, but as someone's reading it, they keep going because every module leads into the next, now they have to keep reading because they are continually pulled through the sales letter. One tiny technique, which you might have noticed – sometimes I can't help but use it in my speaking style – are these things called bucket brigades.

In the old timey past, when a house was on fire, we didn't have fire trucks, didn't have fire hoses, couldn't drop water from a helicopter, we had to go to the lake, go to the river, dip a bucket in the lake, and pass that bucket along down a line until someone could pour the bucket out on the fire. That's called a bucket brigade.

In copy, that means that we want someone to read one sentence, read to the next sentence, then read to the next sentence. That's why sometimes we'll start sentences with phrases like, "Not only that but" and keep going because that helps us out. In addition, people will now read to the end.

We don't want to overdo it, I don't want to sound like an academic here, but so much of copywriting is starting someone at the top and ensuring they read everything down to the bottom. It sounds simplistic, but think about it.

If someone was sucked into your headline, you wouldn't have to worry about your headline selling the whole course. When you put up a headline, below that put a sub-headline. The only job of that headline is to make someone read the headline below it. The only job of that headline is to make someone read the paragraph below that. The only job of that is to make someone to read the paragraph below that.

If someone invests an hour of reading your web page, they go from top to bottom, now they understand everything. They understand that this problem of not being able to play the guitar, of not having an autopilot mailing list, why it's so important. They reach your product, they understand exactly what's in your product, they understand how much is in there, and when we list every component of our product, I love putting a value next to each thing because, if I have a one-hour video showing you how to bring traffic to your website, what's that worth?

Let's say it's worth $500.00 because it would have cost you $500.00 in guess and check if you were trying bad traffic methods. It would have cost you $500.00 using someone else's system. That is definitely worth $500.00. We can say, "The web page template is worth $100.00. The module on making money from your list is worth $300.00." You can total it to be worth $2,000 and say, "But it's not $2,000. Today, you pay $19.95."

Now, it's like a no-brainer because, not only did you grab my attention – that's the attention part, the headline – you identified with my problem – that's interest, problem/story. You explained everything in your product – desire, solution, the product – now I have everything I need. All that's left is the action, referred to in copywriting as a "call to action."

We say, "Here's the price. Here's the guarantee. Go ahead, do it at once. Click the button, your membership will be activated instantly in the next five minutes. You'll be able to log in and watch these videos right away." There we go. That is a web page.

You might be thinking, "I heard somewhere that long copy is dead." You know what? It depends on whom you're selling it to.

Who Are You Selling To?

If you're selling to someone who needs all the information, if you're in a niche such as Internet marketing where you might have this big long course, you need long-form copy.

If you're selling a piece of software, you can demonstrate it in three minutes, five minutes, a video is more appropriate. But you're still going to use a headline. You're still going to relate to their problem. You're still going to explain the different parts of your software or your course. You're still going to tell them at the end to buy.

A sales video is more compressed than a 20-page long sales letter, but it's the same logic. You're making the same arguments, and what I find so funny is the WordPress crowd – people who sell WordPress plug-ins, WordPress themes – they think they want the shortest web page possible. They'll make several columns, they'll cramp stuff on three or four columns, all these funny icons, but when I see something that needs a lot of explaining, like a WordPress course or a WordPress membership site with plenty of plug-ins and themes, they have to make it long-form copy.

What's funny too is, because it's – for example – WordPress, they're heavy on clean, big, giant graphics, it's still a sales letter, but it's like a two-column sales letter, or it's a sales letter with maybe less text than normal, but it's a long, scrolling sales letter. This is what sells.

This is what sells in video, in audio, in person, to make someone take any kind of action. When we have an opt-in page, we're trying to make someone enter an e-mail address, it's short. Blog posts, it's different, but it's the same steps, AIDA – Attention, Interest, Desire, Action. Give them a headline, introduce their problem with a story, have your product with the solution, have that call to action, tell them to buy immediately.

Copywriting Review

We talked today about how to sell anything online using the magic of copywriting. Now, it's okay to be a salesperson. You want to put your best foot forward, you want to make some money, and I think what's helpful is that, instead of hiring a copywriter, You're the best person to explain why your training, why your software, why your product, why your solution is the best that it is, and use some of these techniques that I've shown you such as the bucket brigade, the headline templates such as if-then, the formula such as AIDA, identifying objections, focusing on results, all that kind of stuff. Those are all tools that you should have in your arsenal.

What I tell many others is devise it yourself. Maybe don't write the s yourself but devise the first draft, like my first sales letter – it's a headline and ten bullet points. Improve it using the copywriting tools we've shared today then either hire a copywriter to finalize it, or have them critique it – even better.

Chapter 22: 4 Objections & 4 Alternatives

"Each problem has hidden in it an opportunity so powerful that it literally dwarfs the problem. The greatest success stories were created by people who recognized a problem and turned it into an opportunity."
– Joseph Sugarman

Here's the best way to implement that AIDA, or Attention-Interest-Desire-Action formula:

- overcome 4 objections people might have to your product (in order of simplest to most complex and desperate, without actually mentioning your solution)
- list 4 possible ways of solving that problem (the first way is not having ANY solution, the 4th and final possibility is your solution)
- introduce your solution dramatically, then describe that offer

Objections people have, or arguments for NOT buying your product. You need to be in the mindset of telling a 5 year old to clean their room. Children are good at thinking up excuses. I know, because I once was one!

You tell a child to clean their room. I can't because I haven't done my homework yet. Fine, do your homework. I can't because I haven't brushed my teeth. I can't brush my teeth because I'm out of toothpaste. They can't do this because of this and this and that.

Overcome the Four Objections

We need to reduce this down to the four most common and list them in order of NEWBIE REASONS to MOST AFFLUENT reasons. I'll explain what that means in a minute, but examine these examples:

Let's use "webinars" because we're already on that topic. Four objections people have to running webinars: (1) I don't think I need one, (2) I can't figure out the technology (3) I'm too scared, (4) people might not show up.

Plug it into "weight loss" ... four objections: (1) I don't think I need to lose weight, (2) I think I'll be miserable if I always diet or exercise, (3) every weight loss solution is a scam and doesn't work, (4) I don't think I'll be able to keep the weight off.

Plug it into "stock trading" ... four objections: (1) I don't think I need any money, (2) I don't have millions of dollars to invest, (3) I don't have all the time in the world to keep track of my investments, (4) whatever system I use will probably lose money or won't make money fast enough.

We have to realize that most people coming to our site to buy are newbies. They don't know anything about stock trading, but they have more than a passing curiosity about it. They also don't want to think of themselves as newbies and have "heard it before", why we are tackling 4 objections. Because if we solve one, they're going to have another and another.

I like to tackle objections early in the sales copy because we aren't in sales mode yet, it makes it easy to tell a story, as in, "I started with THIS and that didn't work so THIS and THIS ... here's why

THIS OTHER THING didn't work." The story flows and we're removing the objections early so we don't have to later.

We could stop at listing the four objections then we'd just be the evening news. Here's what I mean. I'll open CNN.com and list the top stories on that site for today. Remember these are all REAL headlines from REAL stories today:

- Parents react to shooting, verdict
- City is largest in US to go bankrupt
- Scratched witness found dead
- Principal missing after lunch deaths
- If you think it's hot now, just wait …
- Golf shot breaks $80K camera

Negative, negative, negative, and negative again. Bad news attracts people's attention. It's gossipy and hooks people. That's fine, but we want to make a sale so let's give them the light at the end of the tunnel.

The problem is that if we jump out immediately and say, "Here's my product …" They'll think, "Ah-ha! You were trying to sell me the whole time and I don't want to change my thinking." But when we complete the alternatives using a logical argument …

Describe the Four Alternatives

Let's think of four possible ways people can solve their current dilemma. Spoiler alert: the first three have serious flaws and the final alternative is YOUR product. A brilliant copywriter named Eugene Schwartz told us that the marketplace goes through four cycles, or stages of awareness:

- **Novelty** (a new solution in the marketplace)
- **Enlargement** (competitors differentiate by being bigger)
- **Sophistication** (competitors differentiate by being more complex)
- **Abandonment** (the marketplace is jaded and competitors abandon ship)

These four stages of awareness go from the newbie to the most advanced, and we're going to list out our alternatives in that order.

- The "novelty" alternative will be the reality of **not having a solution** or possibly not even being aware of the problem
- The "enlargement" alternative will be some solution **that's not the right fit** or too costly
- The "sophistication" alternative will be some solution that's **too difficult**
- The "abandonment" alternative **will be your product** because all other avenues are now exhausted

Ready to try this out on a few niches? I know I am …

Webinars … Alternative #1: not running webinars. Alternative #2: Google Hangouts. Alternative #3: automated webinars. Alternative #4: The Webinar Crusher system.

Weight loss … Alternative #1: figuring it out on my own. Alternative #2: exercise. Alternative #3: dieting, Alternative #4: Your solution.

Stock trading … Alternative #1: trading based on emotion or on "hot tips." Alternative #2: buying and selling based on predetermined goals. Alternative #3: trading based on technical charts only. Alternative #4: Your solution.

This works. If you don't have a storytelling structure you'll be stuck with a blank page or struggle with your story. If you try things like "The Hero's Journey" where you failed, then met a mysterious mentor, then ignored the call to action, then finally did it … you'll have a story that's too long and no one cares about. If you try fancy hypnotic language like "story stacking" five things on top of another, it'll be too confusing. The best way is to tackle 4 objections, then list 4 alternatives.

See what I just did there? I applied this "4 Objections 4 Alternatives" to the problem of writing copy.

Pitch on a Sales Letter or Webinar

It's important that at this point, you bring everything to a screeching halt (for just a couple seconds) and say, look, here it is. Here's my system, here's my course, here's the only thing for you.

Make a big deal out of revealing the NAME of your course in giant letters, hopefully with a logo or a 3D product box.

You spend the rest of that sales letter (or webinar) explaining the pieces within that offer, the modules and bonuses. Be clear with what they're receiving, list all the components again at the end in a single table, total the value, then reveal the actual price.

Then have a button, then tell them to buy repeatedly. Pretty simple.

If you're worried about "length" … I just looked back at a batch of my sales letters. I tend to have my sales letters be about 1/3rd story (whether the sales letter is 3 pages or 30 pages). On a free 1-hour pitch webinar, it's 45 minutes of teaching, then 15 minutes of pitch.

A pitch webinar is more content-heavy than a sales letter, so we use the WWHW format for that – we'll talk about WWHW in a later chapter. WWHW stands for: Why, What, How-To, What-If …

- Why is this thing you're about to show me important? (5 minute introduction)
- What are you going to show me? (20 minute overview)
- How-To solve this problem? (20 minute demo)
- What-If I get the solution to this problem? (15 minute pitch)

You might wonder why I'm fixating on this copywriting and sales stuff so much. It's because the big earners in Internet marketing (even the computer geeks like me) have this selling stuff down-pat so well that we're NATURAL sellers. Always, even in our "casual" content like articles, books, and blog posts. You should be doing this as well.

20 "I Could's" …

I've said repeatedly in this book (and will continue to say) that no one cares that your e-book is 300 pages long, or that it took you 5 years of research to make it. I care about what YOU can do for ME!

This means you have to find a way to make your course not JUST a weight loss course … but the solution to all their problems. They need to think about holding that bad boy in their hands, and about how much it will change their life in the next 7 days, 30 days, 365 days and beyond.

You also need to ask the question, "How much can I fit into this course without it being overwhelming?" To where you're angry for selling it at $100 because that's too cheap. You should be angry that it's $1000 or $5000 because it's too cheap!

Here's what I want you to do. I want you to list 20 things. These should consist of both things they'll receive AND things you'll deliver to them. Let me list "20 things" I could include on a webinar course, as if I had a magic wand. Then I'm going to delete all but 7 when I'm done listing the 20 "I could's" …

1. I could buy a webinar account for them (if they think GoToWebinar is too expensive)
2. I could host, record and produce their webinar recording for them
3. I could show them how to teach a class using webinars
4. I could show them how to pitch using webinars
5. I could give them recordings of all my pitch webinars
6. I could host a monthly meeting to discuss cutting-edge webinar strategies

7. I could have a place to instantly answer all their webinar questions
8. I could deliver a free physical version of the course (book plus DVDs)
9. I could show them how to have tons of webinar traffic
10. I could promote their webinar to my subscribers
11. I could write (or perform) their presentation for them
12. I could give them ready-to-go presentations to plug into their business
13. I could create software that auto-generates a presentation for them
14. I could create a 99-point webinar checklist that they can use anytime they run a webinar
15. I could meet with them just before a webinar to make them excited
16. I could meet with them just after their webinar to give a critique
17. I could bundle some auto-webinar software
18. I could bundle some list building webinar software
19. I could show them how to turn that webinar into a book
20. I could have a directory to connect webinar hosts with presenters

If you know my business at all (I'm not assuming you do) then you know that we've incorporated some of these 20 into our course, combined them with other things, spun yet others into additional products and courses, and as for the remaining items … I still haven't figured out where they fit.

Let's try this again for weight loss:

1. I could provide people with a 30-day meal plan

2. I could ship the tools they need like a blender or fresh fruit if I can find a company that will do it

3. I could connect them with an accountability partner or nutritionist

4. I could arrange for a medical technician to visit and take a blood sample

5. I could auto-generate a custom meal plan based on things like their blood type, age, and lifestyle

6. I could give members a way to track their daily exercise, calorie intake, water intake

7. I could robo-dial my buyers with a motivational message each day

8. I could offer 3 different tracks of training depending if they want to focus on exercise, a slow diet or a crash diet

9. I could create a dashboard for various tasks like removing particular foods from their diet, adding particular foods, or changing lifestyle habits

10. I could add a forum where people could post questions and give daily encouragement from other members

11. I could somehow integrate an iPhone or Android App so people can sync and post their meal updates with one click, and walking and running activity

12. I could "gamify" the site and give people points and badges for milestones they earn

13. I could somehow connect the site with a Facebook app and Twitter app to automatically post updates to their friends when they achieve goals

14. I could ship additional training and DVDs once people unlock levels within the site or achieve their weight loss goals

15. I could run free Q&A days or call-in days as part of the site to answer personal questions
16. I could record a few videos or run some streaming videos where people can follow with my personal lifestyle, exercise and weight loss routines
17. I could create a database referring people to local trusted physicians in their area for blood tests, weight loss medications and further medical advice
18. I could create a database of recipes where people could list ingredients they have available or plan to buy
19. I could add cooking videos so people know exactly how to prepare the meals that I show them
20. I could create a 100-point checklist showing the steps people need to lose the weight they want

You should notice that once we have this list, some things are "must-haves" ... others are "nice-to-haves" and some are "version 2.0" features. We have to approach this with two mindsets ... first, anything I might want to add. Then delete the things you don't have time to add, so you can have that first version out the door as fast as possible. Wave the magic wand, then remove what's unrealistic.

For you to reach your goal, you need to know what your goal is. And when we create websites, have information products for sale, and create membership sites, we need a goal for what we want that version 1.0 site to look like.

Then, it's simply a matter of filling in the pieces.

Way back when I started my Internet business, I realized that when I was focused on finishing it and reaching these milestones, I actually started making money ...

- I started with **freelancing** – creating PHP programs for others and installing plugins on websites ($1,000/month)
- Once I developed these skills, I took the most in-demand services and systematized them into **information products** – "how-to" digital books ($2,000/month)
- These info-products sold a few hundred copies within a few weeks so I created a referral system or **affiliate program** so I could pay others to recommend by products to their lists ($3,000/month)
- Because these sold so well, I continued cranking out **several info-products** ($4,000/month)
- At this point, I figured that if people bought one "learn how to program" e-book from me, they might want another, so I **built a list of buyers** and marketed to them ($5,000/month)
- When I **e-mail my list consistently** my income increased again ($6,000/month)
- By making **video info-products** (showing these tasks in action as opposed to just writing them down) I created products faster and could charge more money for them ($7,000/month)
- Now that I had consistent traffic, consistent sales, a reputation and a list, I could **increase my prices** ($8,000/month)
- I wanted the traffic to keep coming in so I took small pieces out of these products and gave them away free using what are called squeeze pages, opt-in pages, **free landing pages** ($9,000/month)
- I built **upsells** into my download pages and membership sites so people could immediately upgrade ($10,000/month)

And the income just grew and grew from there as I built the list even bigger, found new affiliates and joint venture partners, added software products to the mix, and more. A big breakthrough was simply increasing my prices and asking for the sale. I'd rather sell a lot for a lot, than a little for a little!

Once you gain this ability to "think" money from thin air – have an idea, match it to a marketplace need, create that product, sell it using a sales letter, and send traffic to it – a few things happen.

First, our expenses tend to swell to match our income. We were surviving on $700 a month rent and before we know it there's a $2,000 a month mortgage, $500 a month car payment, $1,000 a month credit card, bill, and so on. Whoops, now I'm more in debt and back into a WORSE survival mode than I was in before!

Second, our tendency is to "put the brakes on" and slow. Woo-hoo, I just made $2,000 dollars, time to celebrate, go on vacation and the next thing I know, I've taken a ton of time off my business. There's nothing wrong with taking a break if your business is making you money while you're off doing other things.

If you can find a way to avoid the usual traps in Tendency One and Tendency Two, you now have what the Beatles called the ability to "write a swimming pool." When John Lennon and George Harrison wanted the money for a new swimming pool, they'd write a new song, receive pay for it, and build their swimming pool.

Mindset is so important both to receive what you want and avoid what you don't want. We can't take it for granted, and that's what we're going to talk about now ...

Part 5: Double Your Time

Chapter 23: Productivity Booster: Decide to Enjoy Taking Any Action

"Don't let the fear of the time it will take to accomplish something stand in the way of your doing it. The time will pass anyway, we might just as well put that passing time to the best possible use."
– Earl Nightingale

It's funny, every time I ask my subscribers questions like: "Where are you stuck at the moment?" "How could things be better?" "If I could wave a magic wand and fix one thing about you to improve your live, what would it be?"

A few people tell me things like: I need to improve this conversion rate by 1% ... or I need to finish this product ...

Most people who respond tell me they have a deeper problem: lack of focus, not being organized, time management, overwhelm, lack of creativity, or lack of productivity ...

Why You Are Where You Are

The good news is these problems are easy to solve. Then why doesn't every one solve them? A few reasons ...

First, it takes a lot of existing time and energy to break your existing habits. You'll actually put more work and effort into staying the way you are, even if it's "easier" to act a different way – more on that in a minute.

Second, it's even easier to regress into your previous self. Think about "that once" you took a morning run, "that once" you went to the gym after a New Year's Resolution, then never went back, "that once" you paid for advertising? Being a productive person is a continuous process, not a one-time event!

Third, you self-sabotage yourself every step of the way. Don't feel bad, all of us do it. I can't go drive to that place because I can't find my phone. I can't lift weights at the gym because I brought the wrong color shorts. I'm going to cut my run short because the battery in my iPod died. I can't run a webinar because that would mean I actually FINISHED something!

Are we agreed then? All of us have a focus/productivity problem, we need to make a PERMANENT change and in a way "outsmart" ourselves to be better … BUT at the same time, we can't "just snap out of it" or "force ourselves to do it" because we won't repeat the process. Here's what you need to do instead …

How to Change Your Own Mind

Let me ask you something, do you enjoy daily going to the dentist, mowing the lawn, and doing the dishes? PROBABLY NOT!

I ask because this last week, I visited a dentist for the first time in 8 years. Don't worry, nothing was hurting, and it turns out I had no cavities. Why did I go? Because it was the right thing to do.

I thought if they find anything wrong … the damage has already been done, at least they caught it before it got any worse, I can stop worrying about it and I'm better than most people because I'm going to have a good attitude toward thing this easy step.

This month, I also fired my landscaper and hired a new one. I've meant to fire this guy for a while. He stopped pulling the weeds, let the bushes grow into the walkways, began mowing the grass unevenly, and somehow managed to break most sprinklers with his lawnmower.

It's something I've meant to do for a while … until one day, I looked out at that misshapen brown lawn and thought, I'm embarrassed to live here. One phone call, hi I'd like to terminate service, do I owe you anything, thanks bye … a second phone call, are you taking on new customers, here's the services I need, what day can you do it, here's my payment information, done.

You can look at that in either of two ways. One way is, "I have to fire this idiot who can't mow my lawn." "Why does my yard suck so much?" "I have to make these stupid phone calls." "I have to shell out even more money."

Or how about this? Everything's been running on autopilot for a while, but it's no longer working out. The landscaper has other business, he has no problem with being fired. Things are broken, but I'll make two quick phone calls to fix it. And imagine how neat, clean, crisp, trimmed and green the yard will look once this new guy comes in and fixes things.

How This Affects You

You know that with an opt-in page you just can't seem to finish installing? That Kindle book you can't finish writing? Autoresponder broadcast e-mail you can't seem to write and send?

Here's what WON'T allow you to do it:

- Thinking you'll do it later
- "Forcing" yourself to "just do it"
- Ignoring the problem or hoping things will just be better
- Being a victim and enjoying your failure

Here's what WILL allow you to do it:

- Deciding that it's the right thing to do
- Find a good reason to do it (even a silly one)
- Separate the problems you need "let go" of and the ones you should tackle directly without delay
- Have fun doing it so you won't think twice about it

And if you still doubt me … have you ever found yourself cleaning your apartment because you had an important term paper due? Because one was more "fun" and pleasurable than the other.

Have you ever washed your car or cleaned the dishes because you were delaying making some important phone call? Exactly.

Look … you can let this behavior guide you in one of two ways: self-sabotage & procrastination (feeling that your unimportant tasks are more "fun" than the important ones) …

Or focused action & productivity. First figure out what important task you need to do, then justify with it logic. And finally rationalize the following things:

- How taking action on that task will give you more pleasure than pain
- How NOT taking that action will give you more pain than pleasure

- How to enjoy taking that simple action, and have fun doing it, so you'll do it now, you'll do it quickly, and you'll do it repeatedly

What's something you've been delaying that you know you should be doing? It's okay if it's something simple, please don't include details if you are too embarrassed ... and what would make you to do it right away?

Chapter 24: Instant Focus (Receive One Productive Hour on Command and Finish Every Task You've Been Putting Off)

"Make what you're doing today important,
because you're trading a day of your life for it."
– Unknown

What if there was an easy way you could not only …

- Improve your presentation, speaking, and product creation skills?
- Create more free content, create more free traffic and figure out what your audience wants?
- Habitually complete all your tasks in one day?
- But at the same time, actually knocked out the most important tasks in your life – even the ones you might have been putting off?

This is a technique I've been using for at least 5 years. It's weird (but easy) to do, and it it's something I use every time I keep procrastinating on a task I want to do, I choose to do, but just can't "bring myself to do …"

- I resize my screen small enough to only have one window open (usually 1024x600)
- I close any distracting windows including Gmail, Twitter, or Facebook
- I RECORD THE SCREEN using Camtasia Recorder (you can use Screencast-O-Matic free), narrate, and "tutorialize" the task that I've been delaying

- I upload that video recording to YouTube with a link back to my site to achieve some extra traffic

For example, I wanted to publish my book to Amazon CreateSpace. But there are many forms to complete with plenty of tweaking involved.

I had to finish it. I didn't want or need to make it ideal, it just had to be submitted!

And here's me fumbling around on Amazon CreateSpace, submitting my first print book:
http://www.DoubleAgentMarketing.com/createspace

I call this the "Camtasia Babysitter" – because you're recording the screen, it keeps you from pausing or becoming distracted by other windows or alerts.

What's one task you could perform, that you know you "should" do, that you "want" to do and even "choose" to do … but now you can record the screen to make sure you finish it?

Chapter 24: Instant Focus (Receive One Productive Hour on Command and Finish Every Task You've Been Putting Off)

Chapter 25: Overcome Self-Sabotage (Become the Person You Want To Be & Return to What Matters)

"Two things define you. Your patience when you have nothing, and your attitude when you have everything."
– Unknown

Have you at some point felt (even for while) like you were …?

- being pulled in different directions?
- that there's just no point in continuing your online business?
- that there's much too much noise, fog, and confusion, so you don't know what to do next?
- that if you only had a better outlook about your daily life, things would be better?
- taking SOME action (like buying a new product, or writing half a blog post) but when you didn't "something" … you slowed down?
- losing all momentum after hitting just one simple roadblock such as what price to charge, what to name your product or what time of the day to mail?
- making too many mistakes to continue this course?

You're in luck, because if you've ever felt like you were in any one of these situations, if you've given up all hope and you needed boost, I think this will help you.

The reason that most of us Internet marketers fail, and keep having to move back on course, is this thing called self-sabotage. If you found it easy to make $500 per month online, but $1000 seems a lot of work, that's self-sabotage and you don't even know it. If you become more uncomfortable the more money you make, that's self-sabotage!

To fix it, I'm not going to give you some cheesy motivational quotes like … "I haven't failed. I've just found 10,000 ways to make a light bulb that don't work." – Thomas Edison

Or tell you silly story after story about how most things were discovered accidentally … (microwave ovens, Velcro, corn flakes, penicillin, all by accident).

I'm also not going to blame you or try to tell you it's all your fault and you "should just snap out of it" because that's not the advice you need to reach where you need to go. What will move you past it? Breaking down the problem so you can identify what "type" of self-sabotage you are experiencing and fix it.

Chances are you experience more than one of these types, but for now let's fix JUST ONE! It's not your fault. You just need to discover which of your sabotaging activities need ADJUSTING.

Self-Sabotage Explained

Here's the thing. Your ancestors were trained to live life carefully. Think about it. If a caveman 100,000 years ago had a fear of heights, he probably stayed away from cliffs and lived to procreate.

Fear of snakes, fear of dogs, wolves, bears, fear of enclosed spaces, fear of the dark … all PROTECTION mechanisms. Back in

242   Chapter 25: Overcome Self-Sabotage (Become the Person You Want
                        To Be & Return to What Matters)

Neanderthal Times, if you found a tribe, made friends, blended, and didn't cause too much trouble, you were far safer than trying to survive on your own.

If things in life weren't quite right, it was "better" to try to adjust to a life of unhappiness, rather than changing your situation ... that might kill you.

Fast forward to the present where more than 99% of the population made of clock-punching, cubicle-dwelling zombies, a "safe" place to be, until you're trying to make a living online, then it's time to fight those survival instincts and take a risk.

It's easier to focus on negative things as a way of NOT taking action and playing it safe, but with these new rules, you're trying to solve your existing problems and in turn you're CAUSING new problems. You're trying to motivate yourself, start a business, make new contacts, create products, and build a list ... all which goes AGAINST your "playing it safe" instincts!

Here are the four forms of self-sabotage that keep you poor. Remember, these aren't just four scenarios I made up ... I've compiled the responses from surveys I've run over the past several years and from other surveys and I've grouped them into parts that make sense ...

Type #1: Priorities (procrastination, reacting, delusions)

Type #2: Habits (drama, slippery slope thinking, Debbie Downer attitude, cognitive dissonance)

Type #3: Emotions (stress, overwhelm, boredom)

Type #4: Meaning (victim thinking, embarrassment, living vicariously)

You'll understand this setup in a minute. Basically, your priorities and your systems are what LEAD you into self-sabotage, your habits cause you to REPEAT that self-sabotage, your negative emotions are the BI-PRODUCT of this sabotage, and the meaning is what you use to JUSTIFY your behavior repeatedly.

Change just one of these factors … you change your thinking and your actions. Identify which of these is your WORST problem and now you're moving towards a positive change.

Priorities

Delusion: You have skewed views of the world, goals, and you're clinging to unrealistic expectations and lies. You either exaggerate or downplay problems with your business, money, self, relationships, or your health.

Procrastination: You let "little everyday tasks" hamper what matters. Maybe you said, I can't do "this" until I have "that" and "that." You waited until the last minute (or even worse, too late) to start, to make any decision, and you didn't think long term.

Reacting: You act impulsively. One crisis starts and you quickly change your entire business, without thinking about the real consequences.

Habits

Cognitive Dissonance: Have you ever thought one thing, but said another? This is called lying, acting, and uncertainty. If you've started a path that you now regret, and you want to change but can't, you might have thought it was easier to "pretend" or continue doing what you're doing ... until you've decided ... I've had enough, I'm not doing, thinking, or saying what I want to do and say!

Debbie Downer: Misery loves company! If your current life situation sucks, it is easier to do the right thing and correct it? Or ... is it more tempting to do the "lazy" thing and focus on everything negative? To tear others down and pull them down to YOUR level, instead of helping?

To criticize, judge, and even become jealous of everything "good" in the world. In a way, you're training yourself to become "happy" when everyone (including you) is angry and sad!

Drama: You're addicted to the "struggle" and feel the need to be in constant chaos to be alive, awake, and have something to do. Either you're the person who starts drama, or instigate it from others, this is your form of sabotage!

Your need to create drama leads to you going down one "slippery slope" after another. If one little thing doesn't go your way, then everything is in shambles. Let's say you were on a careful diet, and on top of that you woke early and made sure to visit the gym one hour daily. But wait! One day, you simply don't have time to go to the gym. Now, what's the point of anything? You cancel your gym membership, eat a gallon of ice cream and scrap your alarm clock.

Emotions

Stress: You worry too much, and you've created problems out of events that haven't happened yet. You overestimated the risk of something simple like sending an e-mail, or making a forum or blog post. Did you waste an entire week "mulling over" a purchase or waste a month "thinking about" taking that trip? Even after you made that decision, you kept obsessing over it ... not just wasting your own time but becoming worked up in the process.

Overwhelm: Isn't it possible that you've let stress become in your way (under-confidence), but in yet other situations, the LACK of stress (over-confidence) has hurt you? You started too many projects, didn't keep deadlines, had no consistent routine, and you might have let others distract you from your target. Which THEN led to stress, procrastination, and bad habits in the future.

Boredom: Also tying back in with cognitive dissonance AND building on procrastination, let's say you started a project 6 months ago and you weren't able to finish what you started. All that time wasted! Plus, it's easier for you to give up on your next project. And the next, and the next! Then it becomes easier to give up, lose focus, and become distracted by other bright shiny objects.

Meaning

Victim Thinking: Here's a weird one. You were taught even as a little child to be selfless and put others before you, right? But what if took it to the extreme and put EVERYONE before you, even when it hurt you and your business? You always put yourself last, which conveniently meant you didn't have to take any action for yourself. Think about it ... it's "easier" to spend all day helping others free, or being a busybody on a public forum, than taking your OWN action, right? That's scary!

Unfortunately, that's not sustainable. You've always put yourself last so NOW it feels like you're always last, everyone is better than you, you've given yourself an inferiority complex.

Embarrassment: You didn't ask for help along the way. You'd "heard" of that before. How hard could it be? You didn't assert yourself, you didn't admit you needed help, and you didn't assert your desires!

Living Vicariously: This is dangerous! Isn't it true that you can watch a TV show or a movie, or even hear about stories from a friend, and feel almost as if you've experienced those things? It's dangerous because it allows others to live your life for you. You don't have to take risks, you don't have to act, just hear stories and your thirst is quenched, right?

Until … you start comparing yourself to others. You think, that person just turned 21. What was I doing when I was 21? They're finishing college, what was I doing then? They just hit the 100k per year mark, they just had their first child, where was I at that point?

I know I promised no cheesy quotes, but this one applies ideally: "Don't compare yourself to anyone in this world. If you do so, you are insulting yourself." – Bill Gates

Here is self-sabotage explained in a table:

	INTERNAL	EXTERNAL	SOCIAL
PRIORITIES	Delusion	Procrastination	Reacting
HABITS	Cognitive Dissonance	Debbie Downer	Drama
EMOTIONS	Stress	Overwhelm	Boredom
MEANING	Victim Thinking	Embarrassment	Living Vicariously

Laying it out on this table helps ME just as much as it helps YOU. Why? Because with self-improvement, there is no such thing as "permanently" fixing any of your problems. It's far too easy to regress into old habits and forget what tools you used to use to make you into a successful person. You'd be surprised at how many successful people, including me, including Lance, still need to listen to tapes or still need to talk to people when we're having a down day or a down week.

How to Overcome Your Problems!

The first thing you need to do is realize where you need the most help. If you try to go out and "stop self-sabotage" … you aren't going to go anywhere. It's like fighting the "war on drugs" … impossible on its own but it is possible to attack one person or attack one area.

Let's say you take one look at that table and you think, my problem is that I'm being a Debbie Downer. That's a habit that affects others so how about, just for today only, I make it a point to not say anything negative? Or if you're constantly overwhelmed, you need to realize why that is and change the actions that lead to that point, such as over-commitment.

Chapter 25: Overcome Self-Sabotage (Become the Person You Want
To Be & Return to What Matters)

If you need to solve one of your bad habits:

- Take a vacation. Take weekends off, go somewhere out of the house, out of town, outside your usual environment, to clear your head
- Attend an event or a seminar. This also takes you out of your usual space, allows you to think and see things differently, and sets you around better role models
- Replace new habits with the ones you're deleting
- Fix just one thing in your life for now, don't try to drastically change everything, because that won't stick!

To fix your priorities:

- Have a better support system. Trusted people like your friends, family, mentor and mastermind
- Go out more. Find a better mentor if your current one doesn't suit you, listen to self-improvement or training audios now and then, and buy an hour of coaching if you are stuck and need help
- Break your problems into manageable pieces
- Make decisions quickly but change decisions slowly

To take better care of your emotions:

- Limit the amount of "toxic thoughts" you have including being jealous of people or "trash talking" others
- Leave your comfort zone whenever you want to make a real change and reach the next milestone in your business and your life
- Remove anything in your life that you feel is dragging you down or holding you back

Chapter 25: Overcome Self-Sabotage (Become the Person You Want To Be & Return to What Matters)

- Push yourself to move outside your "money zone" ... where you earn more money than you normally would and your subconscious tries to put the brakes on your effort and your income

To change the meaning of your life:

- Find an excellent Reason-Why. I've had enough mentors who went from being lazy, to taking real action once they finally had an excellent reason to build a real business and take life seriously. Events like divorce, children, financial hardship, and age ... sprung these people into action. When it hurts enough, you'll make a change!
- Consider the bigger picture, pick your battles and think about the point of view of others
- Combine pleasurable and non-pleasurable activities (I like to wash the dishes while playing music)
- Clean out the clutter

I hope that helps you to move out of your own way and receive everything you've wanted.

Finale: Better Yourself in 7 Easy Steps

"Just do your best work, then try to trump it."
– Walt Disney

I think it's better to identify and recognize when things aren't going that well. In addition, notice when things are going terrific and you can continue moving in that direction.

Anyway, don't want to ramble too much but I'm sure we will. I want you guys to receive these seven steps written without delay. If you happen to have a pen and paper, I'm going to be listing these seven steps repeatedly because, I don't know about you, but I can't stand it when someone says, "I'm going to list these top ten things," and they take ten minutes on the first, twenty minutes on the second, thirty minutes on the third– you never hear all ten, or you have to listen to the entire program to hear all the ten steps.

I'm going to list all seven steps to you without delay then we're going to step through. Become a better person in seven steps. Even if they don't make sense yet, they will once we reach each of them.

- **Step #1:** Decide to have fun doing it.
- **Step #2:** Justify the pleasure versus pain.
- **Step #3:** Have a wonderful reason.
- **Step #4:** Chunk it into four steps.
- **Step #5:** Apply those into your four daily tasks.
- **Step #6:** Light a fire under your butt.

- **Step #7:** Get in to the habit of doing something productive daily.

Sometimes things are called strategies, but they can also be called tactics. Tactics are little, itsy bitsy, tiny, little tactical things that you can do, right? If you're thinking about warfare, I don't know that much about wars and stuff like that, but if you have battleships moving in a particular formation, or making a particular one-prong attack, that is a tactic – a real quick simple thing.

Real quick simple tactics we've talked about in the past are things like smiling, make yourself feel better, make yourself appear better to others. If you're in a situation where you can remember someone's name, or notice someone's name, if someone happens to have a name tag, or someone happens to have a nameplate on their desk, or you know someone's name, few people – even in everyday conversation even with their friends – rarely use that friend's name. That's another good tactic.

Another good tactic is, if you're trying to complete a particular task, have a countdown timer going. I use a program called Cool Timer. All these things are tactics. They're excellent to help you over that little hump. But the problem is that, if you use them too much, like any tactic, or any kind of drug, it loses effectiveness if you do it too much.

Do you know some chain smokers who have to smoke five, six cigarettes a day to maintain that level? If you've ever partied, we've all partied, right? If you drink too much alcohol in a short period of time, you build a tolerance. You have to drink ten beers to have the effect that one beer might have if you hadn't had alcohol in about a month, right?

Chapter 25: Overcome Self-Sabotage (Become the Person You Want To Be & Return to What Matters)

In the same way, here's a good example. Let's say that you walked into a room – we've all been in this situation – where the room was a mess. Maybe it was your room, maybe it's someone else's room, if you have children, or you have a spouse, or maybe there's a pile of dirty dishes. We've all been in that situation where we saw chaos, right?

Maybe it's some of you guys' office. Maybe it's the room you're in at the moment. It's a huge mess everywhere. Now, what can you do? Well, if you were thinking only about tactics, maybe you'd smile every time you saw this dirty room.

If you didn't do anything about it, let's think about what happens. You're feeling good for no reason, good for a while – except you don't actually fix the root of the problem. You're putting a Band Aid on it instead of fixing it, which means that you keep ignoring this problem of this dirty room.

The next thing is that, if you keep doing this too often, your mind, your body, whatever's between that starts to realize, "Hey! You're smiling all the time at something that you know deep down is a bad thing." The smiling doesn't make a difference. Your brain says, "I'm going to start ignoring this whole smiling thing." Next thing you know, the smiling stops working.

When it comes time to actually clean that room, you can say, "I'm going to let myself become overwhelmed and move on to something else." Now, you've begun a pattern of, "Now that's my problem-solving mechanism," right?

"I see something that I don't want to deal with, I'll ignore that. I won't go in that room. I'll go in that room for a second and not notice. I will ignore the problem." Now you're in a crappy situation. Or maybe you'll clean the room, but you'll – if this is a word – "martyrize" yourself – can someone look that up and tell me if that's a real word?

You're what you call a martyr, you say, "This isn't my problem. I'm doing all this work, I'm suffering, blah blah blah," to fix this problem and you derive some sick pleasure, right? You feel good about feeling bad.

It's like the more you suffer, the better you feel. If you're chasing that good feeling, you have to suffer as much as possible. That's really not a good place to be. What's the answer?

The answer is to decide to have fun doing it. This is the first step out of seven. Step one: decide to have fun doing it.

I realize this in different relationships, right? It doesn't matter who you are, we've all heard about the stereotypical married guy. I know married guys, I know married women, I know all these people who've been in long-term relationships – that's also me – but the stereotypical married guy, what is he?

He kind of loses every fight, he kind of does everything he's told, doesn't receive that much reward, and it doesn't sound like that much fun. You always hear this term "compromise" right? What is a compromise? A compromise, to me, is when you have two people who want different things, they meet in the middle, and they're both unhappy.

It's literally a lose-lose situation, right? An example of that might be, I want to watch this channel, you want to watch that channel on

TV, let's compromise and watch something neither of us wants to watch. That's not good, right?

Step #1: Decide to Have Fun Doing It

How do we turn a lose-lose into a win-win? We make it something where we both have a common goal. That is going to work for you whether it's your life, friendship, marriage, business, when dealing with customers, blah blah blah, whatever it is. It's better – instead of compromising where you're both unhappy – to agree on a common goal. Not where one person has to lose one thing and another person has to gain something else, but where you both receive what you want.

Sometimes that means changing what your goal is, that means changing the person you're with, that means changing yourself. But you need to both – if this is making sense – both want the same and that way you don't always have to figure out how to be unhappy, how to meet in the middle, any of that kind of stuff. This even applies for yourself.

All of us have the inner conflict. I was talking about a martyr – an inner conflict, right? You feel good about being bad so you have to feel good and feel bad – it feeds on each other, you become stuck in the same rut, same routine, same cycle, and same pattern – a million different words to say the same thing.

You want to decide to have fun doing it. That means that, if you see a messy room – just to use a metaphor that actually will help you in real life – you see a messy room where you think, "How can I feel good about this? How can I have fun doing it?"

Now an easy answer for me is to switch on music. I see a pile of dirty dishes, I don't want to wash them, but I switch on the radio, I don't even realize that I'm doing dishes. I'm doing dishes, I'm thinking, "Yes, I'm scrubbing stuff, but I'm having fun listening to my favorite songs. This will be over in a few minutes and when it's done, I'll have a set of clean, sparkling dishes."

For me, a really good motivator is when things are clean and out of the way. You only have to look at Apple products, right? Look at iPhone, iPad, MacBook. It's all a one, single, clean kind of thing – that's the same way that you should be looking at.

Maybe you don't want your house to look like an Apple store all clean and neat with glass, but same idea, right? This helps me in so many ways because, let's say that we're talking about food, somehow everyone struggles with their weight. I know that for me, one easy way of not gaining weight, or if I want to lose five or ten pounds, is a real simple answer: to not have junk food in the house, and to have some healthful food in the house.

This works out well for me because, if I'm deciding what to have for breakfast, or lunch, or dinner, and there's something healthful in the house, I'm not going to eat it but I'm going to take one more step towards eating that one can of tuna basically, or using that one block of meat so that's one fewer thing I have to have in my cabinet, in my refrigerator. That is basically me figuring what my leverage is.

What motivates me much is to be relaxed, have peace of mind, complete things, have things out of the way, so that's what I'm going to be going for. It's important that you decide to have fun doing something like cleaning up a room.

Step #2: Justify the Pleasure vs. the Pain

You look at that dirty room, you say, "Here's the pain of not doing it. Here's the pleasure of doing it." You don't have to make it any more complicated than that.

At first glance, the pleasure of not doing it, let's first move that out of the way, okay? The pleasure of not doing it would be that I don't have to do any work, right? I don't have to be sweaty, don't have to put any work, don't have to hurt my back, don't have to waste time, and I can just blow that off.

If you think about, in addition, the pain in not doing it is that it's going to become worse, it's going to continue occupying your mind, and you're going to develop these really bad habits – not bad habits as your parents said, "Go clean your room!" but habits you're going to do repeatedly throughout your life, which is, if you ask me, not a good place to be.

Even when you were young, when you were told to clean your room, what would happen if you did? What would happen if you didn't? If you did, they'd say, "Great job. You can go out and play," or I guess, these days, go play on your Nintendo or your Xbox, whatever. The pain of that would be you're grounded or you have to clean your room anyway.

That would motivate you at the moment. But what happens now that you're a complete adult? Now you have to motivate yourself and look at the bigger picture – look further down the road that, if you leave that room messy, you're not going to feel good, you're setting a bad example, no one else will feel good, you're going to be in a bad mood and that will rub off on to others, so not good.

But it's also not enough to be a martyr, okay? You have to decide to do it, have fun doing it, and figure out some way to justify having that clean house.

Now this applies to you in your business because, if you don't have that sales letter set up, the pain is that you don't have any money coming in from that project, it's still on your mind, and one thing that I didn't realize at first until it took years and years of understanding the pattern is, if I don't have a project launched in a few days, it won't finish it. I'll become distracted by something else, I'll have another unfinished product, and all these unfinished projects that all make zero dollars and actually cost money because I pay web hosting, I pay domain names, I pay for graphics, I pay for these sales letters to be made, I put in all this time, no money, so it's like you're never going to be at 100% efficiency, if that makes sense.

I know that all of us think, "I should have ten products going." Every minute, every second is going to be accounted for, but it doesn't work that way. You can't ever be at 100% capacity because what happens then? Instead of doing four daily tasks as I have told you many times, if you did twenty tasks in a day, you're going to become burned out, you're going back into this downward spiral.

Decide to have fun doing it. The way to reach that decision point is to look at the pleasure versus the pain.

If you want to dive into this deeper, you should – to make it simple – list four things that you know you don't like to do, or four things that you know that need to be done that you should do, but for some reason or another, you've been delaying it.

Off the top of my head, something like having your car's oil changed. How many times have we – I know that for me and most people, when you have your oil changed in most places now, they'll put sticker inside your windshield in your car, right? They'll list sometimes a date, a month in a day, or a particular number like a mileage of your car. They'll say, "Once your car is at 50,000 miles, return for another oil change."

If you think about something like an oil change, the pleasure is not that apparent. It's more maintenance. Maintenance is never fun, is it? Paying $5,000 to have your house fixed, going to the dentist, going to the doctor, going to have your oil changed – we don't easily see the reward to that.

If you think about, even something as simple as filling your car with gas, you don't see the reward to that until your run out of gas. Wouldn't you agree that that would be darn short-sighted if you ran out of gas weekly or monthly?

You let your car gas tank run to zero, you ran out of gas, were stranded, and think about in that hypothetical moment when, if you're driving, you're in the middle of nowhere – middle of a rainy road, or in the middle of a desert – then wouldn't you give so much? Wouldn't you sacrifice quite a bit, or quite a bit of money, to undo that situation? We fill our car with gas, although it's not fully empty, because it's the right thing to do.

Some things in life, you have to do. But think about this. We could think of filling our car with gas as a painful or boring process. But, you're filling your car with gas, you have the satisfaction of, "Now my gas tank's full. Now I can drive X miles. Now I can go on all these other kind of trips."

Once you take the gas filler thing – the nozzle, I guess – out of the thing, plug it in your car, clip the thing, let it start filling the gas, now you have about three or five minutes of alone time. Time to kind of stop, think, wait, and put your life on pause. Some people like to go into the gas station, buy themselves a soda, buy themselves a snack, go and cool off.

But there are so many things in life that you know you have to do. You will have to go to the doctor at some point, maybe soon. You will grow older at some point, maybe soon. It is going to happen so there's no point in becoming worked up about it.

Do your best – I wouldn't say do your best but figure out what's good about this situation, enlarge those, justify those things, and emphasize those good things about every supposedly boring task, and minimize what sucks.

If you go to that gas station and say, "Geez! I'm going to have to pay $50 for a tank of gas. I'll be right back here in a week, filling it again. Geez! The children use the car, they take all the gas, this car gives crappy gas mileage, this gas station stinks, and my hands are becoming all dirty." If you hear me saying it, it sounds ridiculous, but some of you have your little internal voices that say these identical things, hurt you and sabotage you because you don't have the pleasure and the pain calibrated right.

For me, things like having my oil changed, filling it with gas is preventive. Knowing that before time, I can say something that will happen this month, maybe a few times, is filling my car with gas. There's no point in becoming angry about it, becoming worked up about it. Let's find what's good here and now we'll continue to move our lives forward.

Getting closure on those kinds of things helps give us peace of mind. How about this? Refill your car with gas, now you don't have to worry about that gas problem for another few hundred miles, for another few weeks. It'll come up again but it's a five-minute process.

Back in the day, people used to have walk twenty, thirty years to reach the West coast, to reach where they could actually own some land, they'd catch cholera, diphtheria, dysentery, or whatever other old diseases, and maybe die. You know what? You can drive in your air-conditioned car, listen to your radio, listen to your iPod, drive around, and have a good time.

You're living in probably one of the best times possible because, in the past, people didn't live that long. People didn't have such good technology, medicine. In the future, who knows how scary things will be? With nuclear weapons, or nanotechnology, or computers being everywhere, you won't have any privacy. Now is a good time to live.

Anyway, going off on a tangent, so by figuring out whether all this moves me forward in the right direction? "What is the next logical step?" as NASA used to say. If you're driving a car, you want to go somewhere, the next logical step is to stop at the gas station, refill your car, and you can continue to go where you're going.

Likewise, when you're building your business, the next logical step for you might be to launch a new product, relaunch an old product, run a webinar, e-mail your list, you know what that next logical step is. If not, find a mentor to help you, look at your business, and help you along.

Many of these tasks – if you think about it – are really simple, really trivial. Setting up an opt-in page, doing the dishes, filling your car with gas, cleaning that room. You know what? It is what it is.

Everyone has to clean the room, in one way or another. Everyone has to grow older, it's a requirement. Everyone has to submit taxes, death in taxes, right? Everyone has to, if you want a business, pay for web hosting, pay processing things.

Some things in life, you have to do. If you have to do it, you might as well find a way to want to do it, to choose to do it, to decide to do it, and to have fun doing it. You use your imagination, use your logic to figure all that out, and that way you'll live longer and live a lot happier.

Step #3: Have an Excellent "Why"

We've talked about things like setting an example, or being a better person. What you need – an essential ingredient – is what's called a reason.

Here's what I mean. Is your goal to make a million dollars? Maybe it is. Let's say it was, that's great.

Is that a real goal? Do you wake in the middle of the night, or early in the morning and say, "Yes! I am so close to making a million dollars! I am one step closer to making a million dollars!"

Are you excited about the million dollars on its own or are you excited about moving to a bigger house? Paying off your house? Going on vacation? Retiring early? Helping someone else in need?

Setting up a college fund or a trust fund for your children or your relatives, your family?

Being able to relax, not having to worry about money, that's what you're chasing. You're chasing an emotion, a feeling, right? The reason that alcohol, drugs, cigarettes, gambling, and such like are so attractive, people are drawn to them is that of a feeling, because of a rush.

If you've ever won money in a slot machine, at poker, if you've won anything, you receive that rush. It's a short-term rush. I guess the problem is the rush you receive is always a similar feeling, isn't it? It's not like doing drugs versus gambling. It's (0:24:33.6). You do it for that good high, that good feeling, right?

That'll work in the short-term. But you'll end right back where you started from. I think a way better way of doing it is to be more forward-thinking. You can still receive that rush, you can still feel good, but how about you achieve something in the process?

If you win $10 at poker, do you achieve anything? If you light a cigarette? If you become blackout drunk? You receive that feeling, then you're hung over, or you need another cigarette, or even gamble some more, or you were ahead in gambling, now you're behind. You're still chasing that good feeling. But how about you find a way to better your life?

Here's what I mean. One day I was out on a walk – one of many – I walked past this house. It was a two-story house, big, wide, had a cool corner yard, and it was about $500,000. It had palms in front, it had professional lighting where the lights at night illuminated those palms, it was a beautiful house, and what did I do? I grabbed a flyer.

This was at a time right before the real estate blew over, many homes were for sale – not necessarily foreclosed yet but there were many homes for sale because home prices were high. It was a seller's market, basically. People were trying to sell their homes.

I grabbed a flyer, put it on my wall, and after a few months, I had filled an entire wall with different for-sale flyers of different homes that I liked. I looked at all those and I figured out, "I want a two-story house certainly. I don't want a big yard because I don't have a family yet. I want the front room to have this and this. I wanted a look and feel similar to that. I want a garage, not an alley, so I'd park my cars in there, all that cool stuff." That became my reason.

I wish I still had it but I wrote – I had pocket-sized notebook – I wrote what I wanted. I wrote something like, "I want X dollars in the bank." That was okay, but I thought, "What will those dollars bring me?"

I think I wrote, "I want X dollars in cash flow. What would that benefit me?" By the time I got down to number nine or number ten, I listed, "I want this exact car. I want this exact house." There were a few other things in there. I think it's like, "I wanted to go on this number of trips, vacations this next year."

I listed my goals. A year later, I had magically done all those things. I'm sure all those things – I don't have the exact piece of paper but a year later, I had a new car, I had a new house, I'd gone on five or six trips for business – they were all over the country. I had fun, made money, made contacts every time, that was my reason.

I said, "A year from now, I have this, this, this, this." Sure, money was a part of it. I knew money had a lot to do with what that would achieve. But I had a real goal.

It helps you look ahead in the future, and imagine what you'll have. That way, you can rewind to the present and say, "This is what's going to drive me daily." Look at people like Lance whose family, whose daughter drives him – I mean, family for older guys I know is a huge, huge motivator.

Guys who slacked off, didn't do much, but once they married, once they had a child, once they saw a car they wanted, now they put their butt in gear. I definitely don't have all those flyers still, but that helped me nail down exactly what I wanted.

It works, again, with everything. I can think of when I was in early college. At the time, I didn't have a girlfriend. I had some friends, actually, one of those couples who married really young and it was kind of creepy.

I was talking to the wife of this couple and she said, "What are you looking for? What do you want?" "Do you want a one-night stand? Do you want a relationship for a few months? A long-term relationship? Marry right away? How many children do you want?"

I said to myself, "I don't know. I'll take what I can." You know what I "got?" Nothing at the time.

But once I had met a few people, made a few mistakes, been with the wrong few people, who put all the pieces into place and made me realize, "This is what I want. I want this kind of person, with this kind of personality, who has this kind of interests."

I'm not saying an exact template. I'm not saying the perfect person because the perfect person doesn't exist. But a handful of things that you know that you like and things that you don't like so you can identify is this is a candidate? Is this the kind of person? There's not one, there's many, but is this a good fit?

Again, that helps you, not only with your life, but also you look at what am I going to move forward with my business? What am I going to set up? What am I going to build? Now, you can tell, is this what to move forward to? Or is this not to move forward to?

A good way of thinking about this is, if you've ever done any kind of investment, stock trading. There's different ways of investing, isn't there? You can do day trading, swing trading, options trading, you can leverage yourself crazily, or you could buy a boring stock like Pepsi where it stays flat. You put your money in, if you took your money in ten years, you'd have the same sum, only they have these things called dividends, right?

A dividend is, if you have your money in the stock, they'll pay you a particular sum yearly or every quarter for having your money in there. The more money you have, the more they'll pay. That's more a preservation of capital situation.

Sometimes, people will put their money and play both sides. They'll bet for a stock and against a stock at the same time because they want to keep the money they have, maybe increase it, but the goal is to preserve what they have and not necessarily multiply it or turn $1,000 into $10,000.

The decider between that, many times, is age. If you're twenty or thirty, you're going to take a lot more risks because, if you lose all your money, you have the rest of your life to recuperate. Now if you're sixty, seventy, eighty, or ninety, you don't have as many decades left in your life so you want to play it safer and keep the money that spent your life building up.

Know where you're at. That will dictate your goals, what you want, if you've reached your goal, what the next goal is, and what direction to go into.

How about this? List the ten things that you want the most in the world and delete all but four. If you don't know which six to delete – you write ten, delete six, left with four – leave the most emotional ones there, right?

If you listed ten things, if I were you I would list the sum you want in the bank, the amount of cash that you want monthly so you have that written, but make those two good things you delete. What you'll usually end with is – I've pulled my list many times, grouped the most common answers – family, security, travel, retirement, that's pretty much it. Status maybe.

It comes down to the six human needs we've talked about before – certainty, variety, significance, love, growth, or contribution. But we want real physical goals. By physical I mean, if you want a child a year from now, that's one of your goals, now you know what you have to do coming up – marry, look into the fertility thing, stop using birth control, do family planning, whatever, but have a goal, have a reason.

Imagine that picture. Make it a physical or a tangible goal instead of a monetary one. Now, you're not being greedy. You're being clear about what you want because you want to build a better future, have better possibilities like retirement, vacation, travel, or security.

Step one has been to decide to have fun doing it. Step two is justify the pleasure versus the pain. Step three is have an excellent reason, as if you have a newborn, you want to give them a better life, cool. Now, it's not all about you. This whole time, you were trying to make it about you – you felt nervous, you felt greedy, you felt bad – but now it's about someone else. Now you found your own leverage point.

Step #4: Chunk It into Four Steps

Now that you know where you need to be moving forward in the future direction, now you need to actually do it. Take massive action. You've heard this, right? What Lance and I say is, "Chunk it into four steps."

That means that, if you want a recurring online business, you have to figure out a few things. You have to figure out the list, the traffic, and the offer.

Let's say that you're going to make an information product on self-defense. That's always a good example, right? You have the skill, you know all this kickboxing, eye-gauging, crotch-kneeing kind of stuff, you have something good to teach, and you have good information. But you want to make money from it.

That's another thing. If you just say you want to make money, how? What are you going to actually use to provide value? I guess that would be the fourth chunk of it – the value, the list, traffic, and the offer.

You figure out, "How am I going to provide value? What would someone actually pay for?" The answer is, "What do you see around you? What books are on The New York Times Best Seller list? What kind of magazines do you see? What kind of skills do you have? What do you see people charging a lot of money for?"

You don't want to sell a $10 product if you want to enter a niche. You want to sell something where you can potentially charge $100, $1,000, $10,000 if you do it for them. Real estate's a good example because, if you were a Realtor, you'd take someone to a few houses, they decide the one they want, you figure out the agreement, the contract, the bidding, they sign papers, and you take your commission.

You teach self-defense, in the most extreme scenario, you would run a physical live class. You can have people come to your class, pay a set sum, run the class for six, eight, ten, twelve weeks. Every time that there's a lesson, there's training, there's hands-on stuff. At the end, the course is complete.

You need to figure out how you're going to be paid money then figure out – kind of working backward – exactly what that offer is. If you're an Internet marketer like me, it's usually some membership site – membership site could be one-time payment site, payment plan, could be continuity.

But what can someone pay for and what kind of training, what kind of tools, software, and checklists will they receive? What kind of complete home-study course will they receive? Will they receive DVDs? Live webinars, videos, and audios? Most important, what will those videos and audios contain?

You figure that out, that's what's called the offer. Now the question is, how are you going to bring traffic to that offer? Many times, that will be – if you already have a mailing list, if you have contacts, if you have people who can recommend you, you set up what's called an "affiliate program" or a referral program so people can recommend you, appear on Internet radio shows, appear on normal video shows, publish a book, write articles, make videos, set backlinks, post on forums, do all these things that will bring eyeballs back to your site.

You think about, if you're in that certain niche – if you're in a personal defense niche, if you're a fanatic, if you know stuff – you've probably bought someone else's personal defense course, haven't you? If not, go ahead, and buy it. But those courses you bought, the courses you found, think about how did you find those courses? That means you're part of the traffic.

Maybe you went on Google and you searched in that search box to find that course. Now, that means you're going to have to rank for that term or a similar term. That means that after a particular celebrity – maybe not a celebrity but – an expert or guru in that niche, get some interviews with that person, or have that person recommend your product, or figure out how you cannot be competitors but have complementary products.

Maybe you went to some off-line event and you bought from there. Learn how to become a speaker. Become friends with people who run those events. Network and go to those events, work your way up, and prove yourself in providing value. So many people who I've promoted, they first proved themselves to me. They joined my affiliate program, they sent traffic to that, they made sales, it became time for me to promote them, and I happily did it.

Chunk down whatever you have to do into four steps. Chunking will stop you from being so overwhelmed like how we have these seven steps, I've broken them into easy, digestible pieces of you.

Technically, we're not just going over some stuff. It's going through seven easy steps.

Chunk whatever you're doing into four steps – in anything. That's where four daily tasks return into play because, if you're setting up a website, let's say you're setting up a membership site – that sounds like a lot to do. But we say, "I want to set up the back end, the content area, I want to set up the sales letter, explain to people what they're receiving, set up the payment button so they can pay me and receive access, and maybe figure out the traffic, or maybe write some e-mails, make people see it."

Now, we said set up a membership site. Now it's a lot easier because we're setting up little pieces. Now onto step five, an ideal transition to apply those into your four daily tasks.

Step #5: Apply Your Four Chunks into Four Daily Tasks

If you've listened to me for long, you know that I'm not a fan of a whiteboard. I'm not a fan of a to-do list. I'm not a fan of priority projects because, things like projects, all they look at you to do is plan your life a month or two months down the road. A month or two months from now, you might be doing something completely different.

You might have hit a snag or a roadblock, now you're off in a completely different direction. Many times, we distribute our product, we thought it would sell well and it didn't. The reverse has happened. We distributed some quick product, it sold well, and we said, "Cool! Now we're making this money, we're going to devote more time to this, make it better, have more people to see it, and make more money."

Instead of the to-do list, go to your four daily tasks. That means that, if you haven't done that for today, list the four most important things you do today. Not tomorrow, not the next day, but today!

What needs to be done? Not only what needs to be done but what will you enjoy doing? To enjoy doing that, weight the pleasure of doing it versus the pain of not doing it. Look at how can you eliminate the pleasure of not doing it and increase the pain of not doing it, if that makes sense.

Any action you haven't taken, the reason that you haven't taken it is that the pleasure of not doing it is greater than the pain of not doing it and the pleasure of doing it is less than the pain of doing it. I think I got that right.

Everything in your life – every action, every thought, and every emotion – is justified by logic, justified by the pleasure and the pain, so you've got to stack the pleasure of what you want to do and minimize the pain in which you don't want to do. That way you'll act.

A good way to do that is to have an excellent reason, a good motivator that overpowers any other thought. If you have a child, if you don't – I don't know why my brains on children today but bear with me – say you had a child.

The child has a cavity, a really bad one – he's in a so much pain. Now, if you have a child, if your children are all grownup, you don't have one yet, maybe you don't plan them, but someone in your life – let's say an imaginary child that you have, or a real one

– has this exceedingly painful cavity. They're crying, writhing, and almost about to pass out from the pain.

Then, wouldn't you do almost anything to have that child's filling fixed? Make the pain go away, drill that thing, whatever. Fix their problem.

If you were delaying launching that product, had a book done and you're saying, "I don't know whether I should put it out there. I don't know whether I should charge this price. Maybe I should give it away free. I don't know whether anyone can see it. I don't know whether I can e-mail someone to arrange an interview. I'm not sure if I can set up a web page."

Then if you think, "If I didn't set up that web page, it would equal this child being in pain." Now you set up that web page.

Again, if someone had a gun to your head and they said, "If you can't write even the crappiest sales letter, I'm going to shoot you in the head." You'd find a way to do it. You'd justify some way of writing that silly sales letter.

Not a stupid sales letter. That's limiting language. You want to enjoy doing it.

Make a simple web page. No web page is ideal, no web page locks good. I actually, in a way, derive some pleasure with putting out an imperfect web page if you'll let me explain.

Let's say I distribute a web page – kind of ugly, it has some typos, I didn't slave over it, but this one web page makes me $50,000 in a week. I'm going to feel good. I'm going to feel, even with the typos, people loved it.

I can go run a spellcheck anytime I want and fix it up, but even the slap-shod – if that's a word – (actually it is slipshod) web page makes all this money, I must be a good marketer, or this must be a good offer. This must be something that people love.

Have four daily tasks. That way, you'll train yourself. It might take a month or so for you to move into this groove, but do four daily tasks. Don't try them, don't work on them.

Complete four tasks daily, there's always tomorrow to make it better, but at least complete things today. Please! If that means that your logo's not ideal, that's not a problem immediately. Make the best you can do and tomorrow, one of your tasks can be to improve it.

You know what? If you distribute a product with a crappy logo, it still sells, then maybe the logo isn't that important to begin with. You don't know unless you try it, so four daily tasks. That consists of three forty-five-minute tasks, and one ten-minute-task.

Three tasks that each take forty-five minutes and one task that takes about ten minutes. Now, why do I say forty-five minutes? Because those three, I guess, normal-sized tasks sometimes take half an hour, sometimes take an hour. Instead of saying, "Have three tasks of thirty to sixty minutes," plan for them to be forty-five minutes to make it simple."

Sometimes you're going out for the full hour, sometimes it'll be short, but three forty-five-minute tasks, which might be, for me, something like fix a bug in this plug-in, might be record this sales video, might be e-mail ten people to potentially become affiliates, might be to dictate out ten articles – those are all tasks that, on their own, would take about forty-five minutes.

I'm careful about saying things like minutes – forty-five minutes – because I want forty-five focused minutes, okay? We could all take an hour to write one article easily. How? Have your e-mail open in one window, have your Facebook open, e-mail, text messages – you can easily waste most of that hour, and only have one article to show for.

Three tasks of forty-five minutes of focused effort and one ten-minute task because there's always those little things in the day that needs to be taken care of, or, for me usually, that is e-mailing my list. I e-mail my list almost daily because I want to train people to open and click my e-mails daily. I want to keep making money and traffic daily so daily I send out an e-mail.

I know that many time management systems make you either only do the big, huge projects – the big, huge tasks – or only the little unimportant tasks like clean your desk, clean your e-mail inbox. No, I'm talking about three forty-five-minute tasks, one ten-minute-task.

Trust me. I've been doing this daily for years. The system has barely changed. But this is what works for me. I'm talking about tasks business-related, not in your life.

I don't think cleaning your desk is business. That's your workspace, that's your own time. Business is what makes you money. Does cleaning your desk make you money? No.

You can try to justify it and try to argue with me but no. Having to clean your desk, sure, it'll make you more productive. But what can make you more money is buying an ad, right?

Buying an advertisement, bringing people back to your site, improving your sales letter, sending e-mails to your sales letter, setting backlinks – those are important business tasks that will make you more money so do four tasks today and don't plan further than tomorrow on paper.

Today, you're doing the four most important things. You might have in mind, "Tomorrow, now that these things are done, maybe I'll list a few things," but don't fall under that trap. Please, don't do it. Don't fall in that trap of over-scheduling – of scheduling ten things tomorrow, ten things the next day – because, what happens if you miss one thing and it has to shift back? That's never fun.

Do I complete four things daily? No. Most days I do, but some days I only complete two or three things. What do I do with those remaining one or two tasks? They might not have mattered. Tomorrow, I don't do them.

Or they might have been important, which means tomorrow, I'll do them first thing. But if I notice that I keep carrying over these tasks daily, if it happens more than a few days in a row, then you need to complete it immediately or it's not important.

When I say carry over tasks, I mean, tomorrow you're still doing four tasks. If today, you planned for four tasks, only did three, you're not doing five tasks tomorrow. You're still doing four tasks tomorrow. That one thing that you didn't do today, either it somehow fits into tomorrow or you don't it, but trust me on this, have four daily tasks.

Don't plan the whole week, the whole month, just plan today – maybe a little of tomorrow. Keep doing the most important things daily.

Now, how do you make sure that you do these four things daily? You do basically what I would call "lighting a fire under your butt." I guess the stereotype for this would be quitting your day job.

I know many people who kind of glide through life. Maybe they have a cushy job. I know I kind of did, I know Lance kind of did. You end by having two lives, right? You have your cushy, laid-back day job, and you have your business – they're both kind of mediocre, aren't they?

Because you don't put that much effort into your day job, you don't put that much effort into becoming noticed, or receiving a raise, or moving up, or being promoted because you don't need it because you have your Internet business. In your Internet business, maybe you'll launch a product a year, or send out an e-mail a month. You don't put too much into it because you have your cushy day job.

What you've finished by doing is you're working twice the amount, putting in half the effort, and receiving half the results. I'd rather put 100% of myself into that business during business hours. When I'm done, on my times off but I know that I did as much as I could. I made a wad of money, I got a batch of results, I was productive, and I was the best business person I could be.

Many of you need to be at where your back is against the wall, where you have to make this happen. It's kind of sad because many people, it happens where they lost their job. They don't expect it, they're in a panic, and they suddenly have to change themselves – change their behavior, change of a pattern – overnight.

It doesn't work. It's a gradual process. That's why we kind of touch on the same subjects repeatedly because I want to keep you, I want to drag you and keep you on this path because all of us need to continue being a better person. There's no doing it once and stopping because what happens if, say, you're overweight, you worked out a lot, you stopped, went back into old habits, start overeating again, stopped exercising? You're going to gain that weight back – sometimes even more weight than you had lost.

We need you to change beforehand for you to develop good habits that you keep doing, keep enjoy doing, and that keep paying off and improving your life, improving the lives of others.

Step #6: Light a Fire under Your Butt

Light a fire under your butt in a few ways. Like we said, have your back against the wall. Have yourself at where this is the only direction to go. For me, I probably quit my job too late.

I stayed in for a few years. I was not miserable but I wasn't 100% happy with that job. There were limited opportunities for growth, it was a secure job but the pay wasn't as high as it could be. Some of the tasks I had to do were kind of fun, but many of them weren't.

I knew that I couldn't be stuck in that job forever. I visualized myself ten years, twenty years down the road. I knew that, if I were still in that job in twenty years, I would hate myself.

You need a reason to improve – a goal to strive for and a reason that the pleasure versus pain will really help you. You might have to look ten years into the future and say, "I haven't been forward-thinking enough. I've been thinking a month before time instead. If I quit my job now, that's painful because I'll be out of money, have to change, and have to work. But ten years from now, if I had been self-employed for ten years versus at this day job for ten years.

Now, what's the pleasure and the pain? Maybe I don't want to be stuck where I'm at present."

Another tactic that helps with lighting a fire under your butt is this thing we've talked about before called an accountability partner, which means you have someone to report to – not a boss, but more a mentor – more a guide, an adviser.

At the beginning of the day you say, "I've got these four tasks to do," they don't have to know what those tasks are – it's better if they don't because, that way, you don't have to explain it, talk about it, become excited, and talk yourself out of it. As when you told your wife, "I've got to set up this page, send this e-mail, contact five people, and create a graphic." That's all they need to know.

They don't need to know how you do it. They'd probably become bored and hate you for it. Say those four things and say, "At the end of today, can we go over this list in a minute?"

Go through and say, "Did I do number one? Yes. Number two? Yes. Number three? Yes. Number four? No, I didn't. The reason that I didn't is that I hopped on Twitter, got distracted, and ran out the day. Tomorrow, I'll make sure to make up for it, not to contact Twitter – I can contact Twitter when my tasks are done."

You end by feeling good if you got all four things and feeling bad if you didn't.

Finally, to make yourself complete those tasks as you're doing them, use – what we called earlier – a countdown timer. Bring up this timer. I use a program for Windows called Cool Timer. Search it in Google. You can type in 45 minutes. Click the button and it slowly counts down the seconds. That way, you'll stay on tasks.

If you count those seconds and you hopped on Facebook, hopped on your e-mail, you're wasting precious seconds. If it's a real problem, record yourself using screen capture software like Camtasia or Screencast-O-Matic to make sure that you do it.

Step one, decide to have fun doing it. Step two, justify the pleasure versus the pain. Step three, have an excellent reason. Step four, chunk it into four steps. Step five, apply those into your four daily tasks. Step six, light a fire under your butt. Step seven, get in the habit of doing something productive daily.

You know what? I wish that I had a cool acronym for these seven things. If you can think of one from what I listed, can you go e-mail them into **support@doubleagentmarketing.com**? Let me know because I'd like to have a cool way of people memorizing this, or easily return to these seven steps to becoming a better person.

Step #7: Get in the Habit of Doing Something Productive Daily

Get in the habit of doing something productive daily. It's a shame that we're almost out of time there. We're in the final minutes because once you reach the end, now you have to move on to not quit but move on to the next milestone.

Like we said with the weight-loss example, many people put the screws to the wall or the pedal to the metal in for a month, for a week. They have a big launch, they receive money, they make their first big break, make their first little step of progress, and they return to what they were doing before. They say, "That was so much work, it'd be so much work to keep going. Let's just stop. That's easier."

But you need to reach where your mindset is so good, or your head's on straight enough, where because you had so much fun building your business, and because you're going to have so much fun with the results of building that business – the freedom, the money, the enjoyment, and the fulfillment that it gives you – that it actually would be more difficult to go back to your previous self.

Many people in our lives use a thing called "limiting language", but you should phase it out as much as possible – words such as "try," "work," "hope," "I'll get to it," "we'll see," so you know what? I'll try to get that done tomorrow.

What does that mean if you'll try to complete something tomorrow? That means you won't do it. If you're going to finish it tomorrow, you'll finish it tomorrow. Does that make sense?

It's like, what if you tried to set up an opt-in page today? That implies that you failed, right? What if a baseball player tried to hit a home run? That means they didn't. That means they did their best, they put in some effort. But they should have hit that home run.

You're not going to set up an ideal opt-in page. Instead of trying to set up the ideal opt-in page, set up an opt-in page. Tomorrow, make it better, but at least you did something.

When you say you'll work on it, what does that sound like? It sounds like you're going to do something you don't want to do, you'll suffer, it won't be fun, and you won't want to repeat it. But if you do it, you did it. There's no more thinking, there's no more hemming and hawing about it, you did it.

Limiting language and limiting beliefs hurt us as well. A limiting belief means that you had a big launch, you said, "Whoa! I made $30,000. That's enough. I'm comfortable. I'm not going for $40,000 because what if I don't? I'm not going for another $30,000 because, if I don't hit my goal the second time, I'm on the decline. If I do hit my goal the second time, I'm struggling to maintain."

Once you hit your small achievable goal, you want to move to the next goal. That's why monetary goals are good, but are also dangerous. I think a good goal for you is to launch your product and make fifty sales. You make fifty sales, your next goal isn't to make 100 sales.

Now, you make product number two. It's good that we hit that milestone. I'm going to do what I can to make a bundle of more sales, but now the goal is to sell a product that's twice the price. We're not going to feel like a failure if we don't sell as many. We're not going to feel like a failure if you don't sell a thousand, but now we're going to move in what? The next logical step. Do the next thing.

Your life is always becoming better, but in different ways. It's not a straight line.

You might have a month that's $30,000. The next month might be $10,000. The next month might be $40,000. It's not a straight line. It's a kind of roller coaster. But look at this too, you're building a list, you're training your list to buy from you, you're contacting different partners, different markets, different affiliates – you are always moving in that forward direction.

You do have to, like we said, light a fire under your butt so you are always doing the right thing and moving forward. But you don't want your goals to work against you. You don't want your goals to attack you. That's why we need to do a few things like a pattern interrupt, which means that we're changing our state, we're looking at things differently.

I can tell you that once, we did a launch, and in about a week and a half we earned $17,000. I felt bad. I was like, "Geez!" We didn't make a million dollars, we didn't make a $100,000, and I talked to someone making a little more money than I at the time.

He said, "You know what? You did well. Most people can't make $17,000. Instead of focusing on what you didn't do, or focusing on that $17,000, well, now what? What's the next thing? What's the next piece of software you'll make? What's some other different goal?"

What's some other goal, or what can you purchase? Maybe you'll purchase a new couch, new furniture, new house, and new car from your next launch. That way, you still reward yourself, you still had more pleasure than pain from doing something bigger and better, but you weren't setting yourself up for failure.

I think a role model, a mentor, or someone guiding you – telling you what to do, or being proud of even your small successes, not rewarding your failures but being proud of your small achievable goals – to help you out.

As we're winding this down, I want to share with you three quick stories about some one-hit wonders because I want to make sure that you don't, again, you don't want to fall in to this trap of being a one-hit wonder, of changing your life. Yes, it is uncomfortable at first. I can tell you it wasn't comfortable at first running webinars, creating products, even talking for a long time and not having anyone talk back to me – this was awkward at first. But now, it's super-smooth, it's super-easy.

I know if I stopped for even a few weeks or a month, it would be awkward, it would be a struggle, it'd be a lot more work returning back. All of us know people who expend way more effort and energy not doing things, or staying where they are than just moving out of their comfort zone because it is uncomfortable, but it will turn you into a bigger person.

Guess what? Even if it were horrible and terrible, at least you now know what you want to do and what you don't want to do. For some people, if they did a launch, they made $50,000, they went back to their previous self, which means the $50,000 wasn't that important to them. Money wasn't their real goal. Their real goal was having a stable life, that's fine.

But let's be honest here. Like figuring out what you want in a partner, in a spouse, there's certain things you want, certain things you don't want, now you will certainly end with something unexpected. You're not going to receive exactly what you planned, but at least you'll know whether it's a right fit.

Real quick, three one-hit wonders. A mentor of mine, this British guy, set up AdSense sites. Many times he'd set up a site and make a few thousand dollars from the site with Google Ads on it. In one weekend, there was a charity concert with Madonna, maybe Kanye West, Eminem, and Bono – it was a huge international event, he set up a site for it a month earlier, put Google Ads on it, and that site got so much traffic because of organic SEO that he made

$1,500 from two-cent and five-cent clicks in a weekend because it got so much traffic and it got so many advertisements.

But what happened after that weekend? The event was over and the site wasn't even worth keeping the domain name around. This guy built it up to where he was making about $2,000 a month from five and ten-cent clicks on Google AdSense doing nothing. But one day, his site got Google-slapped and he lost all his search-engine rankings, lost all his traffic, therefore, lost all his clicks.

Overnight, went from $2,000 a day – I think it was – to $50 a day. He got so angry, instead of adjusting and fixing it, or making more sites, or figuring out what to do differently, he deleted his sites. Most people would have said, "Geez! A few dollars a day doing nothing? That's still worth it." It's doing literally nothing and he had to put in time and energy to reduce his income. Not that good, right?

Here's someone else. Someone else hung out on an Internet marketing forum. A prolific poster posted a cool idea to find thirty experts – thirty Internet marketers – and interview all of them about how to make, I think, $100,000 a year. That was the prompt.

This was years ago, this was before any kind of interview product had ever been made for Internet marketing. This was years and years ago, you probably wouldn't even recognize this guy now.

He put this idea out. Another guy saw the idea and actually implemented it. This other guy, also gone from the Internet for years. He contacted all these guys, some said no, some said yes – after he got a few yeses, he went back to his notes and said, "This, this, this, and this guy said yes so, if you don't accept, you're saying that they are better than you if you don't participate in the interview."

He sent out this e-mail of ten, twenty questions. These people wrote for five, ten pages so they wrote this book for him. He just had to contact these people and now, because he got all these popular names, the book sold well because all these popular names were on there, he made $100,000 in a month from this launch, and what he did was then said, "I'm a huge success," and began charging $15,000 to $20,000 to make products and make sales letters,.

Now the problem was, he was a one-hit wonder. He didn't know what he was doing, finished by taking these people's money, and not doing anything. He set himself up for failure.

He didn't know what he was doing, charged a wad of money for it, listened to the mentor, and once he was overwhelmed he hit that one obstacle – that one roadblock – he panicked and fled. If he came back, I'm sure a few people still recognize him, he'd have a difficult time making a business boat moving again.

He didn't even try! He just left! A $100,000 in a month is good but, if that's your only money coming in for a decade, now it's suddenly not so good.

Third and final guy, I promise as I point to the third and final guy, distribute an offer where, for $300, he would make an e-book product, he'd make a sales letter, he'd bring traffic to it, send e-mails, put it up on SEO, attract affiliates for it, put up traffic exchanges, and guarantee – I want to say – $1,200. Guaranteed quadruple the investment.

What happened was he made, I think he made 100 sales in a few days, what does that come out to? $30,000 in a few days? Not too shabby. But what happened was, he also promised a return on investment, in itself kind of scary, wasn't expecting so many sales, and I think promised a turnaround time of a week or two.

What happened was, he only had time to focus on one or two products, put most of the money down to hire a product creator, hire a copywriter, hire a traffic person, and the product finished by not being so good. The product was aimed at the wrong audience, it didn't sell that well, and just didn't give people their money back. That person asked for a refund, he said, "No, I'm still working on it." Person put in a chargeback.

Now, that money was frozen. The other ninety-eight people, I should say, also were saying, "Hey! Where's my product? You've done nothing. You've focused on these other guys." They've all put in chargebacks, got his account frozen, and now he was stuck again because he couldn't even access the money. He couldn't even pay people to make these products so he couldn't deliver, couldn't turn the money, and now he actually lost money on this venture, had to go and hide.

What's the commonality with these three people? They didn't think things through. They were confident but they didn't actually follow through. They didn't start small, they grew bigger, and once they hit that one little roadblock, they fled and ran away.

Here's my opinion on it – the first guy, the AdSense guy, should have done a few things. Should have, first, decided to have fun fixing the problem because, if he got Google-slapped, his competition did as well. Here's an opportunity to teach his techniques – another mistake he made.

He didn't teach his system. He was scarcity-minded and thought, "If I teach my techniques, everyone else could be like competitors." Yes, but the Internet is big enough for all of us. If he had a membership site and this Google stuff happened, if he had solved the problem, he could have devised Version 2.0 of his product, or his membership site, and now got a wad of money and doubled it.

Many times, I'll do something and teach how I did it. But I'll make more money – I'll still make money doing it, but I'll make even more money teaching how I did it than doing it. It's like, am I going to dig a hole? Or am I going to sell shovels to dig holes? That was one thing.

Now, the interview guy should have stopped with what was working. He figured out how to make $100,000 in a month. Could everyone write a book at that? Was that a lesson that's sellable? No. But now that he built a list of buyers, he found a product that was a hot seller, make the next product of that type and sell it to that next audience.

If he had found a way to have fun doing that, he would have done it day long. He would have kept repeating it and repeating it.

Now, the problem I saw with the product creator guy, the only problem with the offer was, if I could give you $300 and you could quadruple that in a month, why don't you do that on your own? In that person's situation, I would have systematized that.

I would have said, "I have an idea for a product, I'm going to market it, and that way, I could make a product that I know will sell and I don't have to fight with a client. I'll hire all these people and systematize it. Now, I'll be able to figure out a repeatable way to quadruple my investment. I won't be under a time crunch, won't have to deal with clients, customers, chargebacks, and deadlines. I could do it at my pace. Again, once I have it systematized, now I can sell that system."

Maybe I can sell it better for you. Maybe I could tone down, maybe I won't promise a return on investment, but I'll apply this is what's worked for me, and they can pay $300, receive all this stuff that would cost them $3,000 otherwise. A sales letter, a product, traffic, but it's not about investment. I won't get in trouble in that way.

I think there's always a solution. I think, if you're always looking for not how to give up, how to pass or fail, but, if you discover an obstacle, how do I now fix that obstacle? How do I now reach that solution?

Many times, I've distributed typos on sales letters, sent out the wrong e-mail, bungled webinars, and continued because it's never the end unless you choose for it to be the end. Even if you had a failure, you can pick yourself on and move along.

How many times has Donald Trump failed or declared bankruptcy? How many products has Apple computer distributed that weren't that good? Many if you look around. Microsoft, I'm sure you can think of a ton. Windows Millennium. The Apple III, the Lisa.

Ford, a motor company, distributed the Edsel car. They could have said, "Finally, we're at the end," or "It's time to change my direction. It's time to either change my goal or change my actions. Now reach where I want to be, get in that habit, and do these things daily. Become a better person."

Now, it's actually more work, more effort, to go back to that person you were. Whereas before, it was comfortable to stay this person who didn't finish a lot, now that you've transformed yourself into this new person, it's like you were out of your comfort zone in the transition period, but now that you're this new person, to return to being basically – let's say – a loser, you'd have to move out of your comfort zone to return to that point.

We do have to look at ourselves honestly, Not in a way that's being mean to ourselves but, if you're off-track, if you're being a jerk, notice that and know when you're having a problem.

Become a better person in seven steps.

Step #1: Decide to have fun doing it.

Step #2: Justify the pleasure versus the pain.

Step #3: Have an excellent reason.

Step #4: Chunk it into four steps.

Step #5: Apply those into your four daily tasks.

Step #6: Light a fire under your butt.

Step #7: Get in to the habit of doing something productive daily to make sure that you're moving in the right direction, you're not wasting time, that your life is becoming better daily, you're moving forward in the direction that you need to be, and you're moving away from the bad stuff – what you shouldn't be doing.

That's all from me, Robert Plank. Go out there immediately. Make me proud. Become a better person in seven steps.

About Robert Plank

Robert Plank runs a million dollar business on the Internet creating information products, software tools, and webinar training.

He can show you how to not only save time in your business and everyday life, but do more in less time. Master WordPress. Build your list. Create passive income from information products. Generate residual income using membership sites. Scale and talk to use audiences using webinars. And more!

Robert's Online Presence:

- Blog: www.robertplank.com
- Podcast: www.robertplankshow.com/itunes
- Fan Page: www.robertplankshow.com

Robert Plank's other titles on Amazon.com:

- 100 Time Savers: Start Less, Finish More, and Cut 10 Minutes a Day from Your Schedule to Gain 60 Hours of Free Time Per Year
- Article Crash Course: Get Published, Get Instant Authority and Become an Expert in Any Subject
- Double Agent Marketing: Live the Double Life, Control Your Destiny and Become a Self-Employed Entrepreneur By Starting Your Own Home-Based Internet Information Business
- Four Daily Tasks: Overcome All Internal Roadblocks Using a Few Simple Rules, Solve Any Personal Problems and Keep Moving in a "Forward" Direction in 10 Easy Steps

- Internet Marketing on Crack: Master Your Time Management, Marketing, Sales, Traffic, Products, Customer Relationships & More From Just a Few Simple Breakthroughs
- List, Traffic & Offers: The Internet Marketing Profit Shortcut
- Membership Cube: How to Create a Passive Income in Just a Few Simple Clicks
- Secret Conversations with Internet Millionaires: How to Make Money Online with an Internet Marketing Business
- Sell on Amazon FBA: Easy Steps to Create an Online Passive Income Amazon Business with Retail Arbitrage & Private Label Sourcing
- Setup a Point & Click Website Today: Install WordPress, Create Massive Content, Secure and Backup Your Blog WITHOUT Being a Computer Geek

Robert's courses:

- Membership Cube: setup a recurring membership site
- Income Machine: establish your online system including your blog, traffic, opt-in page, autoresponder sequence and more
- Dropship CEO: sell physical products on Amazon.com
- Make a Product: self-publish a book (physical and digital) on Amazon.com
- Profit Dashboard: earn money from Fiverr
- Podcast Crusher: create your own podcast

Discover more about him at RobertPlank.com/about and contact him at RobertPlank.com/ask if you have a personal question, want to appear on his podcast, want him on your podcast, or if you wish to enquire about availability for speaking engagements.

www.ingramcontent.com/pod-product-compliance
Lightning Source LLC
Chambersburg PA
CBHW051444170526
45166CB00001B/104